LEEDS UNITED
ON TRIAL

LEEDS UNITED ON TRIAL

*The Inside Story of an
Astonishing Year*

DAVID O'LEARY

LITTLE, BROWN

A *Little, Brown* Book

First published in Great Britain in 2002
by Little, Brown

A CIP catalogue record for this book
is available from the British Library.

ISBN 0 316 86065 4

Typeset in Plantin by M Rules
Printed and bound in Great Britain
by Clays Ltd, St Ives plc

Little, Brown
An imprint of
Time Warner Books UK
Brettenham House
Lancaster Place
London WC2E 7EN

www.TimeWarnerBooks.co.uk

Contents

To chairman Peter Ridsdale, the board of directors and all genuine Leeds United supporters.

Introduction

Hindsight is a wonderful thing for an author reflecting on a series of tumultuous events that occurred over the course of twenty-three months. In this book I have aimed to be honest in detailing these events as they happened at Leeds United. It has been a time of varying emotions, with moments of glory inevitably tinged by other issues, in particular the trial of several of our footballers at Hull Crown Court.

Obviously I have had to be sensitive to the notion that the legal system does not stand still. I wrote almost all of this book before the retrial of Lee Bowyer and Jonathan Woodgate began in October 2001. That prevents me from being wise after the event by altering my earlier attitudes to the case or by climbing on to a high horse and suggesting that 'I told you so'.

I cannot stress emphatically enough that I found the attack on student Sarfraz Najeib absolutely appalling. I am satisfied that my feelings of abhorrence towards that senseless violence are clearly conveyed in these pages. I stand by my belief, and the view of Leeds United, that if any of our players had been found guilty of grievous bodily harm they would never have played for the club again. Paul Clifford, the man convicted of carrying out the attack on the young student, deserved to be sent to prison for his crime.

The arrest and trial of four, then three and finally two Leeds United players actually stretched across three football seasons, all of which were tainted by the notoriety created by the conduct of the players. As well as answering to the court, they will have to answer to me for their behaviour.

This book is dedicated to all the kind, caring and, in many cases, ordinary people whose lives were affected in some way or other by the events surrounding Leeds United over the past couple of years. In particular I must mention my own family, who have always cheerfully tolerated my commitment to football and who in recent times have been towers of strength when I have needed them to be.

My family provides the firm foundations on which I have always based my professional life. My wife, Joy, may have no real interest in the game but she has been a rock in supporting me and guiding me through my career as a player and manager as well as performing heroics in the upbringing of our children John and Ciara, for which I am deeply in her debt.

Joy can be withering in her condemnation of the sums of money football clubs spend on player transfers as well as the salaries on offer within our industry. She believes that at the top end of the wage and transfer scale the figures quoted are obscene. Living for the past twenty years with a wife who is not impressed by the opportunities for fame and fortune all around her has been marvellous for me, because while I know I have the absolute backing of both Joy and the rest of my family, at the same time they never indulge me.

Introduction

I am proud of the O'Leary family roots. I'm not ashamed that I grew up in a small Dublin flat in which I shared a bedroom with my parents, brother Pierce and sister Emily. Life may be different for us all now, but that sense of family and the experience of growing as a unit has formed me. I want the players at my club to believe they are part of an extended family. I want them to honour the standards we set for them and to respect my leadership.

I do not walk around wearing rose-tinted glasses. I know we cannot expect young players to live like monks. Every club has a code of discipline and nobody can demand that their players are teetotal saints who shun the limelight. The lure of nightclubs, of freeloading friends and potential notoriety, has tempted footballers down the years. Unfortunately, too many of them have taken the bait and squandered their talent.

The rewards on offer to the best footballers have never been as great as they are today. A career in the top flight should ensure that they are set up for life financially. The wisdom of protecting and prolonging their lucrative careers by living sensibly and following the latest proven guidelines on alcohol intake and diet would seem blatantly obvious to most people, yet still we witness examples of gross misconduct off the field involving drunken footballers. It is a bewildering problem, and one I know we cannot shy away from at Leeds United.

I hope you enjoy reading my thoughts on a period of history at our football club that is probably unprecedented. There has been no guidebook to management for me to turn to along the way, and no manager has headed down this route in quite such challenging circumstances.

I am grateful for the absolute support I have received from Leeds chairman Peter Ridsdale during our time together. I often joke that he drives me crazy as we go about our daily business, but I also know that he has backed me to the hilt every time I have asked him to find the funds for player recruitment. I could ask for no more from a chairman-manager relationship and I can also say, hand on heart, that I like him as a human being as well.

I am well aware that as one trial at Hull Crown Court ended, another began. In the years after the publication of this book, Leeds United as a football club will remain on trial in many people's eyes. We have to live with that responsibility. My dream since taking charge at Elland Road has been to build a modern club capable of winning trophies in England and competing on a regular basis in the Champions League. That dream remains intact.

1

A Bright Tomorrow

When I accepted the job as Leeds United's manager back in October 1998, I recognised the two critical challenges I had to overcome. The first was the obvious test of a manager's acumen: can he send out a winning team? The experience I'd already acquired at Leeds working alongside George Graham as coach and assistant manager, allied to the knowledge I'd accumulated through my own playing career, made me confident I had grasped how winning teams come together and prosper. The winning ethic isn't based on a mixture of magic wand on the training ground and good luck on the day. I was aware from my playing days at Arsenal, as well as from the restructuring George had done at Elland Road during the previous couple of years, that hard work was the real foundation on which progress would be made. Only by cultivating the correct attitude among the players and then offering them guidance on the best way to fulfil their collective ability could I expect to enjoy any real impact as a manager in my own right.

But winning alone was not enough for me as I set myself the goals on which I wanted to be judged as the new Leeds manager. I decided I had to take on a task of epic proportions. Some of my friends thought I was crazy. They said I was kidding myself if I thought I could pull this one off. The challenge was this: I wanted to transform the whole image of Leeds United Football Club. I wanted Leeds to establish a global reputation as a team that played attractive, attacking football and was positive in going out to win games, not to kill them.

I have immense respect for the way the late Don Revie built Leeds United into a modern football power during the sixties and early seventies. The Revie legend lives on at Elland Road, and the years his sides spent in contention for honours every season, winning plenty of silverware along the way, are testament to his great vision as a manager. But if we are totally honest, we have to accept that Revie's was not a team that won the hearts and minds of the sporting nation. For all the wonderful memories our fans quite rightly celebrate – the remarkable victories over some of Europe's top clubs, the passing routines that left the opposition chasing shadows – words like 'cynical' and 'brutal' are never far from any discussion of the Revie years among unbiased football people. Take Johnny Giles, for example. He was a terrific player, but he was renowned for going over the top in tackles. I didn't want that from my team. I wanted players as great as Revie's, but I wanted us to be known as a competitive side that played thrilling football.

I had a vision of a new Leeds team that would delight real football fans all over the country. I wanted to win over the neutrals. I wanted the television companies to feel they were assured of an entertaining programme when they covered our matches, and I knew that greater television coverage could get the message across. In the mid-nineties Kevin Keegan's Newcastle had been on the brink of achieving the kind of reputation I was aiming for, but after Kevin left the Geordies his empire had begun to crumble. It was said at the time, though, that Newcastle had become everybody's second favourite team. Fans had their own first loyalty, but after that they liked watching Newcastle, cheering on Kevin's boys because of the way they played the game. My ambition was to create the same kind of buzz around the city of Leeds as Kevin had inspired on Tyneside, to renew pride in the local club – and not just because we were the home-town outfit, but because we offered our supporters exciting football. I wanted match day to be a real event for the fans so that, having been to Elland Road to see us once, they would be back again for more.

The public perception of the club was one issue, but there was also a desperate need to preach the gospel of a new Leeds to those within the professional game, in particular the outstanding young British and Irish players around whom I hoped to build my team. In 1998, the players already at the top preferred to ply their trade at more fashionable clubs, and when a burgeoning talent became available on the transfer market, there was no real hope of Leeds emerging as irresistible suitors, or even that the youngster would consider moving to the West Riding of Yorkshire.

So the difficulty of the task I had set myself was not to be underestimated. It would have been easy, of course, to have stuck with George Graham and joined him as his assistant when he took over as Tottenham manager, and he did give me that opportunity. But my appreciation of what Leeds had to offer was fundamentally different from George's. For him there was no comparison between the size and potential of the two clubs. He felt he'd taken Leeds as far as they could go, and that all roads now led to White Hart Lane. I respected the fact that the Tottenham job brought him closer to his lovely wife, Sue, and their Hampstead home, but I didn't agree with his assessment.

George's last game was the first-round UEFA Cup defeat of Maritimo after a penalty shoot-out. We drew Roma in the second round, and George joked that he hoped we'd have our new boss before we had to take on the Italian giants with Zdenek Zemen in charge. When George left I was made caretaker manager. After our game against Leicester on 3 October there was a two-week gap in the fixture list during which it seemed likely that the club would appoint a permanent replacement. Every day brought a new rumour of who it would be. Coventry's Gordon Strachan had his supporters until Martin O'Neill, then at Leicester City, emerged as the clear favourite.

For that first game against Leicester I left things pretty much as they were, reasoning that as my spell in charge would be a brief one, there wasn't much point in disrupting the side. But when we lost I realised how wrong I was, and vowed that if I was still in control for the following game I would put the O'Leary imprint on the team. I heard that the players were saying that I'd gone easy on them, and knew I should have told them what I really thought. I promised myself that next time – if there was a next time – I would be heading home on the coach believing in what I had done that afternoon. I wasn't going to go for the safe option again.

I was still at the helm when we faced Nottingham Forest at the City Ground a fortnight later. I told the players I felt I had let myself down against Leicester, and that I was going to pick a team I really had faith in, even if it proved to be my last game in charge. I left out Lee Sharpe and a few others and selected youngsters like Jonathan Woodgate and Stephen McPhail. I explained in no uncertain terms to Jimmy Floyd Hasselbaink that I felt he had been talking a good game since his return from the World Cup finals in France the previous summer. I had been to Portugal with George to see Jimmy playing for Boavista before we bought him. He had developed into a great goalscorer

4

for Leeds, but suddenly, he seemed more talk than action. I took the opportunity to let Jimmy know where he stood, and he was shocked. The players began to see the real David O'Leary. If I was going to do the job I was going to do it my way, and there was no question of simply going through the motions. If I was surplus to requirements, I'd walk out with my head held high.

The management issue was still unresolved when we went to Rome to play in the UEFA Cup. The board chose to stay in a different hotel from the team. I sensed a sheepishness among the directors. It seemed to me that they were distancing themselves out of embarrassment at not having given me the job. On the Monday night Martin O'Neill's Leicester met Tottenham, the club George had just taken over, in a televised game. The rumour was that Martin would make this his farewell appearance at Filbert Street, wave goodbye to the Leicester fans at the end of the match and join Leeds on the Wednesday, when we were back from Italy.

George called me in Rome on the Tuesday to wish me all the best in our game, and told me he was sure Martin would come to Leeds. Apparently, after the match the night before, Martin had asked him for his opinion. George had said it was the most magnificent job at a brilliant club with an unbelievable chairman and fantastic money. George laughed as he suggested that in hyping Leeds to Martin, he was doing me a good turn – since I clearly wasn't going to be named as his successor, Martin's appointment would give me a route out.

Although we played really well we lost 1–0 in the Olympic Stadium. We were getting on the plane home on the Wednesday when the news broke that Martin had signed a new contract at Filbert Street and was staying. Like George, I'd thought he was a cert. A few of the lads started teasing our chairman, Peter Ridsdale, with digs like: 'Thanks, Peter, for the new contract you got Martin.' All of a sudden, the situation had taken on a different complexion. As we stepped on to the tarmac in Leeds the chairman asked me: 'Where are you going to be tonight? Can I come and see you later?' I told him I'd be at home. Later that evening Peter arrived with Jeremy Fenn, the managing director at the time, and we spent an hour and a half discussing the situation. They said that, after my three weeks in charge as caretaker, they had decided that the man they wanted for as manager was me, and made me a formal offer.

I must admit I was pleasantly surprised – I really hadn't thought I would land the job. When George left I thought the Leeds fans might turn on me and tell me to follow him back to London. In fact, my son John had been concerned enough about the likelihood of this happening to stay away from our game against Leicester City for fear that the crowd would give me stick and make it clear they didn't want me. Incredibly, though, the opposite happened. The supporters had saluted me even though we lost 1–0, and by the time we played Nottingham Forest two weeks later, opinion polls showed that I was the choice of 90 per cent of Leeds fans.

Surprised I may have been, but I wasn't at all fazed when Peter Ridsdale told me I had the job. I'd always wanted to be a manager, and I knew I was ready to try my hand at it. I'd already weighed up the pros and cons and thought about how I would handle it. Now I had a golden opportunity to prove my worth.

I signed a two-year contract with Leeds, but I'll admit that at the time I wondered if I would last beyond that season. I thought the club might make a move to prise Martin O'Neill away from Leicester the following summer. I took some flak, too, for landing a Premiership job in my first managerial appointment. I remember Gabby Yorath, the television pundit, writing in a column that Leeds was too big a club for a first-time manager and that, like her dad, Terry, I should have learned my trade in the lower divisions. Quite a few others took the same line, and I was generally branded a lucky boy.

A Bright Tomorrow

I asked Eddie Gray to be my assistant manager. Eddie was of course one of the heroes of the Don Revie era and had himself had a spell as manager in the 1980s after Leeds were relegated from the top flight. He had returned as youth-team coach during Howard Wilkinson's reign and had been promoted by George Graham to coaching the senior players. That night Eddie and I shared a bottle of champagne to celebrate. Neither of us could ever have predicted what lay ahead for us.

I felt George Graham's view that Leeds could climb no further up the football ladder at home or abroad was mistaken. He was dubious about some of the young players but I had worked with them in training, and I was sure they had real talent. Of course, the likes of Harry Kewell, Jonathan Woodgate and Ian Harte were young and inexperienced, but I knew that, given the right chances and support, they could develop into strong Premier League players.

George wasn't convinced. Once, watching a training session, he turned to me and asked: 'What do you see in Alan Smith?' He was clearly concerned that the young, blond striker was overrated at the club. But I saw him as one of the brightest home-grown talents in English football; a boy with a hunger to succeed that set him apart from the rest, a boy blessed with an innate ability to score goals of all kinds that could be truly breathtaking. A boy blessed with a team ethic and a loyalty to Leeds United that meant he would bleed for our club and stand up to the most vicious attacks from opponents. Smithy the Leeds hard man takes more physical stick than most strikers, but he never moans. I have likened him in the past to Mark Hughes, and I am sure that the great Sir Alex Ferguson, who coined the perfect description of the former Manchester United and Wales striker, would agree that Smithy deserves to inherit it. For, like Sparky in the eighties and nineties, Alan Smith is a 'football warrior'. He asks and receives no quarter.

We had a squad of quality players, but we needed to reinforce it with talent from outside the club. Nobody, however, could have accused me of panic-buying: that is something I have strongly resisted during my brief career. Jimmy Floyd Hasselbaink left us in 1999 in a £12 million move to Atlético Madrid, and we spent a year searching for a new centre forward. A similar situation was to arise in 2000–01 as a result of injury: at one point, after we were thrashed 4–0 by Barcelona in the Champions League, our dressing room was more like a casualty station. But the replacements being offered to us, or nominated as potential signings, were just not good enough for the Leeds cause. They would have arrived, filled the team as stopgaps and then been left kicking their heels when our real stars returned. I knew I had to look to the long term and plan a real strategy, not go off on a short-term spending spree that would simply squander my transfer kitty.

The bottom line on Jimmy's departure was that he wanted more money – more than this club could afford. He thought I could sanction any salary increase he wanted, and told us that if he didn't get what he was asking for he would never play for us again. He believed he was a special case. Dealing with this scenario, and making it clear exactly where I stood, was important for me as a young manager. I rated Jimmy highly. He is an exciting player and a great goalscorer with probably the hardest shot I've ever seen. But Jimmy's agent told Peter Ridsdale, that he wanted his client to be our highest-paid player, and on top of that to receive a bonus for playing and a bonus for scoring, all of which I felt were unacceptable in a team game.

So we made a stand on this issue and we lost Jimmy. We had hoped that Michael Bridges and Alan Smith would learn from him, but instead they were asked to form a new attacking partnership with Harry Kewell while we looked for an experienced, powerful front man. Our quest finally led us to Celtic, where we bought Mark Viduka for £6 million in the summer of 2000.

A Bright Tomorrow

I would have loved to have kept Jimmy at Elland Road and eventually to have paired him up with Viduka, with the likes of Bridges and Smith competing for their spot. I knew he would score goals in Spain, and I wasn't in the least surprised when he maintained his scoring form on his return to the Premiership with Chelsea. But you cannot allow one player to be miles ahead of the rest in the pay stakes, and we wouldn't do it. So Jimmy realised he had to move on, and he knew where he was going.

Viduka was a powerful centre forward blessed with breath-taking skills for a man of his size. We had compiled extensive scouting reports on him before I headed north to watch him play in a Glasgow derby. On the night I saw him he actually missed a couple of good chances, but there was no disputing his qualities. He has good ability on the ground and great feet. He may look chubby, but I was assured by people in the know that he didn't carry an ounce of fat. He is his own man with his own opinions, but by all accounts he was well liked and popular. I realised he was a bargain at £6 million, especially considering the prices being bandied about for other strikers at the time.

I was spotted on my scouting mission to Glasgow and many people assumed that it was Mark's team-mate Henrik Larsson who was my real target. But I was searching for a man to lead our attack and to provide the pivot for others to play off. Viduka was perfect. He had originally caught my eye playing for Croatia Zagreb in a European game against Newcastle before he moved to Celtic: a big, burly striker who was anything but a hammer-thrower. I noticed how great he was at holding up the ball and playing people in. The detractors who argue that he carries excess baggage should see him stripped off. Mark's body-fat level is fine, and with special training at Leeds has climbed to new levels of fitness.

Mark loved Celtic and their fans, but he was keen to play in the Premiership. We got permission from Celtic to speak to him, but it wasn't all plain sailing. I wanted to make the deal as simple as possible but there were five other clubs involved, including Bayern Munich, Deportivo La Coruña and Fiorentina, and we had to sell Mark the new Leeds. Happily, he decided he wanted to be part of it.

By this time Celtic were, of course, being managed by none other than Martin O'Neill, and as luck would have it, while the Viduka negotiations were in progress Martin and I were working together as part of the BBC's commentary team at Euro 2000 in Belgium and Holland. Football can be a small world.

Mark can be impetuous at times, but he takes pride in himself and is always well mannered. He also has plenty of time for people. Wherever we go around Europe, you'll see him sitting in the lounge of the team hotel, chatting away and listening to the views of others. When we played Lazio in the Champions League he bumped into a Catholic priest from Croatia in our hotel, and whenever we had some free time you'd find Mark deep in conversation with the priest. I remember introducing him to my parents in Dublin. He took them to one side in the hotel, sat them down and made the time to talk to them as well.

Viduka's presence, power and goalscoring ability gave us some admirable attacking options, but a key issue I had to address was the potential absence through injury of David Batty in our midfield engine room. I decided we needed an experienced central midfielder who could win the ball and pass it. I went to watch Olivier Dacourt play for Lens in France and was impressed by what I saw. On 2 May 2000, I flew back to France with my chairman to negotiate a deal. I remember the date well because not only was it my birthday, it was also, unfortunately, the day that Grand Prix driver David Coulthard's plane crashed in France. You can imagine my wife Joy's panic when she half-heard the announcement on the news – especially as the Leeds team had already been involved in one plane crash, two years earlier at Stansted. She couldn't get hold of me for some time because we had only just taken off when the story emerged.

Thankfully, I arrived safely in Lens, while David Coulthard overcame his ordeal to compete in the Spanish Grand Prix the following weekend. But, tragically, the two pilots on his plane that day lost their lives.

In his Everton days Olly Dacourt had earned himself a reputation for getting too many bookings, often for impetuous challenges. I'm always wary of managers who claim they can change players and manipulate a lad's approach to the game. That kind of attitude can blow up in your face just when you think you have pulled off a masterstroke in terms of improving a player's disciplinary attitude. But I felt that some of Olly's tackles at Everton had been rash and that he could learn to gauge situations better. He's a competitive lad who always wants the ball, but he needed to show greater judgement in deciding when to commit himself to a tackle, rather than just steaming in there in a gung-ho manner. I had spoken to Everton manager Walter Smith about Olly while my coach, Roy Aitken, had a chat with their assistant manager, Archie Knox. We also talked to John Collins at Fulham, who had spent time with Olly at Everton. We were told that he could sulk a little bit and be a touch moody, but that he was a good professional with a will to win.

Olly had only been back in France for one season, but he really fancied another spell in England. However, it took some tough negotiations to clinch the deal at the right price. The chairman and I spent an afternoon playing bluff with the French club's representatives, threatening to walk out unless they agreed to the £7 million price tag. They wanted a lot more, but we refused to pay it. In the end our tactics succeeded and we got our man at the right price. I knew Olly was a good signing. I wanted him to operate in midfield alongside David Batty, or perhaps to challenge David for a place in the side. I knew he was a better player than the likes of Alfie Håland and David Hopkin, who we had sold.

The third important purchase we made that summer was Dominic Matteo. His £3.75 million transfer from Liverpool became complicated when, during our thorough medical, we discovered that he had a knee problem. A closer examination revealed that Dom would need five weeks of rehabilitation work before he could see match action. It was typical of our injury fortunes at the time. Here we were spending good money on a new player to ease our problems only to find that he was injured, too.

I realised there was no point in killing the deal because I really wanted Dom and, after all, he would be ready to play again in a few weeks. It wasn't a career-threatening problem. I telephoned Liverpool manager Gérard Houllier, a good friend, to explain what had happened and to discuss the options. Dom still wanted to join us, so Gérard agreed to split his wages with us while the lad stayed at Elland Road, got to know his new team-mates and settled into the Leeds way of things. It was an excellent compromise.

I had been watching Dominic for a couple of years and was impressed by his versatility. He was a left-sided defender who could operate at centre back or, if necessary, push forward and show his talents on the left of midfield. Once we got him fit, that flexibility was extremely valuable to us in our continuing injury crisis. Dom did well in midfield in difficult circumstances. He filled in at left back when Ian Harte lost form, and towards the end of his first campaign with us he combined with Rio Ferdinand in a magnificent partnership at the heart of our defence. I have fallen out with him on occasions. I blasted him on the night we beat Lazio in Rome in December 2000. It was the first time I'd had a real go at him, and perhaps he took it the wrong way. His idea of close marking was different from mine, and I felt he could get nearer to his man. I said so after the game, and maybe there was a bit of sulking, but I made it clear that he shouldn't feel I was being personal – I was simply making a constructive criticism for his own good. Dominic is a great lad: he's fit and runs like a real athlete. He takes pride in his game. He won't let anybody take liberties with him, even in training, and he has proved an invaluable signing, especially for £3.75 million.

Some players these days do seem to take constructive criticism personally. When I was a youngster at Arsenal, being taught my trade by coach Don Howe, if I did something wrong he would be right in my face, the blood vessels in his neck bulging. He could tear paint off the walls with his verbal abuse, but you learned quickly under his tutelage. But the days of ranting and raving at players and throwing teacups around are probably over. I know I have lads who feel that any severe rollicking should be administered in private rather than in front of their team-mates. However, there are times when the whole group has to see that nobody is immune.

Top-level football has changed in many ways, and the terms of reference for every manager have changed with it. It is no longer just about winning trophies: the ultimate goal of every big club now is to be in the Champions League every season. One effect of the new system of priorities has been the demotion of other competitions. I love the FA Cup, for instance – its traditions, the knock-out format, its capacity to produce unforgettable moments – but the road to a great day out at the Cup final, winning the famous old trophy and the exhilarating lap of honour round the pitch has to take second place now to qualification in Europe. As a manager I have to accept that my job is to ensure that Leeds make the Champions League year in, year out.

The style with which we cut a swathe across Europe in 2000–01 was the most compelling justification of my desire to transform Leeds United's standing in world football. Our attacking play and our friendly, open approach to the foreign media delighted them, and journalists from all over the world

turned up at our Thorp Arch training ground to interview my
players and me about the impact we had made on European
football's leading competition.

We were inundated, too, by letters from English football fans
wishing us well. Many wrote that they had hated Leeds in the
past but liked this new, young side. The fact that the biggest
single group of correspondents saluting our approach came
from Tyneside, home of the side whose aspirations I'd emulated, was a source of great satisfaction to me. The Geordies
were at pains to point out that they were totally committed
Newcastle fans, but, they said, given that Newcastle hadn't
made the Champions' League that season, they wanted us to
win it. It was wonderful to read, the fulfilment of the massive
challenge I had set myself less than three years earlier.

Attendance figures at Elland Road compared with those of
the Revie days were further confirmation to me that we were on
the right track. In 2000–01, we broke the one million mark for
only the second time in the club's history. Our average home
attendance was 39,016. In only one season of Don Revie's glory
years did Leeds boast a higher average gate: in 1970–71, when
the average home attendance peaked at 39,252. And back in
Don's days, of course, the ground had a greater capacity. Elland
Road might not have been the biggest stadium in English football, but it had vast areas of terracing. In March 1967, an
all-time record 57,892 people managed to squeeze in for an FA
Cup fifth-round replay against Sunderland. One of the
inevitable side-effects of the legislation brought into force in the
wake of the Hillsborough disaster of 1989, which required top-
flight clubs to have all-seater stadia, has been a reduction in
attendance figures, except where a club has embarked on extensive ground-improvement programmes, as Manchester United
have done. When Leeds United won the League Championship
in 1992 the average home gate was just 29,459. We have
increased the capacity of Elland Road since then to 40,200, but

it is gratifying to see that the contemporary Leeds team is attracting 10,000 more fans than the 1992 title-winners. Even when Don's side lifted the club's first-ever Championship crown back in 1969, the average gate was only 35,693. And an interesting footnote to Don's reign is that in his early seasons at Elland Road, before the glory years saw a dramatic upturn in the size of the crowd, average attendances were under 14,000.

But just when our exploits on the field of play were beginning to earn the accolades I craved for my club, the shadow of a trial involving several Leeds United players threatened to destroy all the progress we had made. To appreciate the impact this had at Elland Road, before reliving the highs and lows of the 2000–01 season, we need to turn back the clock to 12 January 2000 . . .

2

'Have a Few Days Off, Boys'

Four players arrested, two fans killed and a football club to guide towards honours at home and abroad. These were the matters preoccupying me in the spring of 2000, and it was an experience that can only be described as harrowing.

The tragedy in Istanbul, in which two Leeds United supporters, Kevin Speight and Christopher Loftus, were stabbed to death while following their team in Europe, stunned football fans all over the globe. It is impossible to condemn vehemently enough the kind of nationalistic hysteria that can provoke an attack on two men concerned only with watching their beloved Leeds play Galatasaray in a UEFA Cup semi-final. The deaths in Turkey followed the arrests that shattered the balance of a season in which we had emerged as outsiders for the Premier League title. I am not saying we would have won the Championship, but I am certain that we were capable of giving

Sir Alex Ferguson's omnipotent Manchester United a real run for their money. What cannot be doubted is that the arrests undermined our campaign in 1999–2000.

Without wishing to make this book sound like a dry, legal document, there are certain facts that we need to put on record. In the early hours of Wednesday 12 January 2000, paramedics were called to an emergency in a side street in Leeds city centre. They found Sarfraz Najeib, a student, lying on the pavement in Mill Hill. His face was fractured in six places and his leg broken. He bore teeth marks from a bite on the side of his face, together with the imprint of a shoe left by a kick or a stamp.

Various groups of Leeds United players were in the city that night, and whether or not they were involved, and the degree of any involvement, in the attack became the focal point of a police investigation. What was not in question was that footballers Lee Bowyer, Jonathan Woodgate and Tony Hackworth were eventually charged, along with Neale Caveney and Paul Clifford, two friends of Woodgate's from Middlesbrough, with causing grievous bodily harm with intent to Sarfraz Najeib. They were also charged with affray, while Woodgate, Clifford and Caveney, together with Leeds United defender Michael Duberry, were charged with conspiring to pervert the course of justice.

In the early part of January nobody could have foreseen the stress and heartbreak that lay in store for us on the streets of Leeds and Istanbul. On the field of play we were doing so well. We'd had a tough fixture list and the players had produced some superb results, including an outstanding 5–2 FA Cup victory over Manchester City at Maine Road on the second Sunday of the month. I felt the lads needed a break, and the season was taking its toll on me, too. I was suffering from a bout of flu and stayed away from the team on the eve of the City Cup tie. I didn't think I'd make the game at all, but I got myself to Maine Road by car, though I felt absolutely awful throughout.

After the Maine Road triumph we had a blank fortnight with

no games, thanks to Manchester United's controversial appearance in the World Club Cup in Rio de Janeiro. We did consider taking the players away on a sunshine break, but it wasn't my preferred option, and with Manchester United pictured strolling along the Copacabana Beach in Brazil while back home they came under attack for withdrawing from the FA Cup, I thought it wiser to give our players some time out at home with instructions to stay with their families and rest. Yet what occurred in Leeds in the early hours of that Thursday morning was exactly the kind of incident, fuelled by excessive drinking, that you know can happen when you take a group of young men abroad. It was the risk of something like this that I'd expressly been seeking to avoid by staying at home.

The first I knew of it was when the players returned to training on Monday 17 January, when there was talk around the club that something untoward had taken place. The next day I was told that the police wanted to speak to Lee Bowyer and Jonathan Woodgate about an incident.

Police officers turned up at the training ground early that morning and said that they wanted to interview the two players. I have to say there was an element of *The Sweeney* to their approach. I felt they could have acted with greater discretion and arranged through Peter Ridsdale or me to talk to Bowyer and Woodgate. After all, the players were never going to run away and hide. Instead it seemed that the police wanted to recreate a touch of the old television programme starring John Thaw and Dennis Waterman. Furthermore, it was apparent that sections of the media knew about all this before we did. This was an issue that was to raise its head again during the first trial, and I will return to it later.

I called the two players into my office at the training ground, a pleasantly spacious room with a formal desk where I normally work and a triangular conference table for hosting more relaxed meetings. This was business of the most serious order, so I sat behind my desk and told the lads to sit opposite me. I wanted them to know that they were facing the boss. I was quite straightforward with them. Looking back, I don't think they could possibly have believed that this was an issue that was going to be brushed under the carpet and forgotten about. I simply asked them what the hell was going on. They immediately protested that they had not been involved in anything untoward and insisted that arresting them was ridiculous. I was expecting a denial, but they protested their innocence with some vehemence.

I knew that several players had been out on the town that night so I made further inquiries. The results were disconcerting, to say the least. We seemed to bounce from one extreme to another, with declarations of innocence being followed by arrests. One young lad called Tony Hackworth, for example, admitted he had seen the incident, claimed he had done nothing wrong and yet six weeks later, he, too, was arrested. Throughout, however, the lads continued to categorically deny any wrongdoing.

We tried to get to the bottom of it by appointing a private investigator to work on the case. The information he uncovered was passed back to me, and I would then summon the players for another meeting at which, confronted with another bit of unwelcome evidence, they would reluctantly own up to some knowledge of some aspect of the incident. As the detective came up with another piece of the jigsaw, the players would concede a fraction more. When they admitted that they had had a few drinks, I told them that I wouldn't tolerate players of mine drinking to excess. A break from training was for rest and recuperation, not for getting smashed out of their heads and cavorting on a pub crawl.

Leeds is the biggest city in England, and yet, with only one football club, in some ways it's like living in a huge village. Everybody recognises the players. It's not like London, where celebrities can hide. Our footballers stand out, and if they misbehave the whispers or complaints come flying back to the club very quickly. They are paid a lot of money to perform as professional athletes, they are ambassadors for Leeds United and they are role models for youngsters. They have to be aware that other people scrutinise their behaviour very closely because of their fame.

Under oath during the first trial, Woody confessed to drinking seven or eight pints of vodka- and rum-based cocktails. Bow, although not a regular drinker, said he had had five or six glasses of wine before arriving at the nightclub where the trouble was brewing. I think they are both better off without alcohol, and the repercussions of that night out only emphasise my point. Balance in life is essential. Advice on diet and fluid consumption does alter, and I know I cannot make my players live like monks, but they must have a balanced diet and a balanced lifestyle. There is a time and a place for footballers to enjoy themselves, but enjoying themselves should not consist of getting drunk out of their minds. There is an attitude among many English footballers that having a good time involves precisely that. I'm trying to educate our players otherwise, a programme that includes employing on our full-time backroom staff a sports scientist who spends much of his time explaining to them the importance of what they eat and drink. He tells them what alcohol does to their bodies and explodes the myth that players can run off the excesses of booze in training.

We are not the only club where players have been caught drinking heavily, and I'm sure we won't be the last. We have to continue to do everything in our power to open their eyes to the perils of drink, not just in terms of high-profile incidents, but also with a view to prolonging their careers at the highest level by sensible living. Even if it had not been linked to this court case, if I had discovered the level of boozing that had gone on among my players, I would have called in the offenders and made it clear that I found their behaviour totally unacceptable.

The working environment at Leeds changed dramatically following the arrests. I would walk out for training and discover that one or more of the players – and not just the lads who had been arrested – had been invited to meet the police to provide a statement. Trying to plan training was a joke: you never knew where you stood. I am not suggesting for one moment that we should have received any special treatment because we are a football club – I'm a great believer that all people are equal, especially within the eyes of the law. But some communication and co-operation from the local police would have helped. Instead I got the impression that if they could put one over the club they were keen to do so. I couldn't escape the feeling that at times the process was being driven by a misplaced idea of political correctness and an eagerness to make the most of an opportunity to bury two high-profile Leeds footballers.

I had seen a similar attitude during my time with Arsenal, when Tony Adams was charged with drink-driving. I don't condone what Tony did, but in court, where I was a character witness for Tony, there was a definite feeling that in the pre-Christmas campaign against drink-driving he would be dealt a heavy punishment as a warning to others. A player shouldn't be allowed to hide behind the protection of a football club but by the same token he shouldn't be made an example of because of who he is, either. All I could do for Tony was to tell the court how I found him as a man. I wasn't asked to fulfil the same role for the Leeds players, but if I had been I would have told the court how they were around the training ground – and as a manager, I never had an ounce of trouble from either of them.

My gut feeling that there was a political undercurrent to the Leeds case was reinforced when the police announced, a few days after the incident, that they were treating it as a racially motivated attack. Weeks later they withdrew that slur, but the damage had been done. This change of mind merited only a single paragraph tucked away on an inside page of the newspapers, whereas the original story had been splashed all over the front pages. I still receive letters to this day from correspondents under the misapprehension that there was a racist element to the offence. During the first trial, both the judge and the prosecuting counsel made it clear that race was not an issue in the case, and yet there were those close to the victim who seemed determined to peddle the race card.

Let me make it absolutely plain that there is no hint of racism at Leeds United. You need only look at our training ground to see that. There you will find Clive Brown, our black masseur, massaging Lee Bowyer and Jonathan Woodgate on a daily basis.

You will come upon our reserve-team winger, Harpal Singh, a Leeds-born Asian, chatting and laughing with Bow and Woody. When Woody made his first public appearance in the reserve team after the trial, it was Harpal's shoulder he was leaning on out on the pitch at Villa Park as he did his stretches. That wasn't a set-up, it was totally spontaneous. Young Harpal will tell you that integration is completely natural at our club.

I buy players and employ staff because of their talent and qualifications, not on the basis of colour or religion. I want players of all races to improve our club. Racism is abhorrent to me, and I have personal experience of the poison that seeps from that appalling concept of mankind. When my parents came over from Ireland in the fifties and looked for bed-and-breakfast places to stay they were met by signs reading: 'No Irish'. Many years later, when I was trying to make my way as a footballer with Arsenal, I came up against the same attitudes. I remember walking into a snooker hall in north London and being told to my face: 'No Irish allowed here. Piss off.'

I have lived in England for the past twenty-nine years putting up with taunts of 'Paddy, go and dig the roads.' So I know what it's like and I would never allow it at any football club I was associated with.

The fact that this kind of mindless abuse is perpetrated by perhaps 1 per cent of the population doesn't make it acceptable. At football matches I actually get more of it as a manager than I did as a player. I suppose I'm a sitting – or standing – target in the dugout during a game. And I will tell you one thing: whatever racist insults have been hurled at me I have never seen a police officer step into the crowd to arrest the idiot screaming at me.

My suspicions of a political agenda were intensified by the debate surrounding the date of the trial. In September 2000, after the players had been committed for trial, the Crown Prosecution Service said that their case would be ready for January 2001. Leeds United's lawyers had pointed out that if the trial took place during the season, the club would be 'severely penalised in financial terms from the loss of a number of players as defendants in the case, and to a lesser extent as witnesses'. Mr Justice Henriques decided to delay the court appearance until June 2001, explaining that the club's representations were one of the factors he had taken into account in choosing to wait until the end of the football season.

Suddenly we found the decision taken by a High Court judge called into question. Lord Dholakia, a Liberal Democrat home affairs spokesman and former adviser to the Judicial Studies Board, said that he would be 'seeking an explanation' for the delay from the lord chancellor, Lord Irvine. 'I'm shocked and surprised that the judge should take into account representations of that nature,' he said. 'It is wrong because if justice is delayed, it is denied to people who are striving to find the courts will deal adequately with cases of this nature.'

Mr Justice Henriques responded: 'Any company chairman making representations of this nature would have had them considered by a judge in the setting of a trial date involving a number of that company's employees.' However, he said that the principal reason for the date he had selected was fitting the trial

23

into the court calendar: the new legal term beginning that autumn was too early and the Easter term too short for a trial expected to last six weeks, which left only the Trinity term, beginning in June 2001.

Nevertheless the judge's decision was overturned and the date was set for 29 January 2001. I imagine that the defence legal teams must have realised from that moment that the politicians would continue to involve themselves in the business of the courts.

Immediately after their arrest I was under pressure not to select Bowyer and Woodgate. There was an outcry in some sections of the media that until they cleared their names they should not be picked for the Leeds team. I have always respected the principle of English law that a person is innocent until proved guilty. The players didn't have to prove their innocence: it was up to a court to establish their guilt on the basis of the evidence. We have seen other high-profile cases involving football people over which there has been so much public debate that the man's crusade to prove his innocence has gone by the board. Remember Dave Jones, the former Southampton manager now in charge at Wolverhampton Wanderers, who faced harrowing sex charges. In the end he maintained his innocence, fought to clear his name and emerged totally vindicated, but not before he was pilloried in the press.

I was disgusted by the crime committed on Sarfraz Najeib. I was just concerned that the involvement of two footballers seemed to be adding to the case an extra dimension that some people relished. I was shown evidence of the number of similar incidents that happened in Leeds, and most other English cities, every weekend, but which attracted very little attention. The only difference with this one was the names of well-known sportsmen on the charge sheet.

As it turned out, by the end of the 1999–2000 season both Bowyer and Woodgate were left on the subs' bench, but that was because the numerous meetings between the players, their lawyers and the players' families were beginning to take their toll on their form. I never considered ruling them out of selection. The time for the club to take a decision about their futures was if and when they were found guilty. In the meantime it was inevitable that they would be baited by opposition fans. There were taunts about them 'going down' and which prison they might end up in. I told the lads that thye had created this problem for themselves by being on the streets late at night, and that they would have to live with it. Even if they hadn't committed the awful attack, their conduct left them open to the accusation of involvement.

Fans nowadays are more fickle and impatient than they've ever been, and the people who run football seem to feel the need to appease them. That, at any rate, appeared to be the reasoning behind the Football Association's announcement that Woodgate and Bowyer would not be selected by England while they were under arrest. I was staggered. To me this was another act of political correctness. And I couldn't help feeling that it was an easy way out for them. If David Beckham or Alan Shearer had been in this situation, say before they headed to the 2000 European Championships in Holland and Belgium, would they have been treated in the same way? I firmly believe they would not. If a court case involving Beckham had dragged on like this, would he have been effectively left in limbo over the course of three seasons? Of course he wouldn't. The Leeds Two were expendable. This was the New FA in action. There were elements of New Labour in the way it formed its policies. The spin doctors were guiding those policies and they were clear about the lines they were following.

Kevin Keegan was the England manager at the time of the arrests. He told Peter Ridsdale that he would have loved to have selected Bowyer and Woodgate for international duty but that his hands were tied. I know Sven-Göran Eriksson would have picked them if he could have done. Bowyer would undoubtedly have merited selection throughout the period following his arrest. Woody's case was different. He is a magnificent player who should be an established England international, but once the trial got underway in January 2001, his form collapsed.

During the police investigation the club decided that if the players were found guilty of the most serious charge, aggravated grievous bodily harm, they would not play for Leeds again. It was undoubtedly the right decision. The only thing I questioned was whether Leeds might end up being punished twice for it. If Bowyer and Woodgate couldn't play for Leeds, and we had to release them, I didn't want our rivals picking up these players as free agents. Why should a less scrupulous club benefit from our principled stand? I felt that we should only release the players for a fee to compensate us for our loss.

Given the work Leeds United have done in the community and the strides we have made on issues like education and racism, the trial was the worst thing that could have happened to the club. In Emma Stanford we have a community affairs manager who is a prize asset to Leeds United. I don't think the players realised just how much work Emma and her department had done and what they were jeopardising through their stupid drunkenness.

The hate mail started long before the trial. It was directed at Peter Ridsdale, the accused players and at me. The two players' agents weren't targeted. The fact that I stood by the Leeds Two by picking them for the team seemed to inflame some people. But why the cowards who revelled in sending anonymous letters filled with bile and threats decided to select my wife for special treatment I will never know. I found that tactic thoroughly disgusting. What the hell had this trial to do with my wife? I made my feelings about this clear to the players, too. It may not have been intentional, but through their boozing and misbehaviour they had dragged my family into a situation with which they were totally unconnected and I was aggrieved about that.

We live in a sick world, and some of the letters I received must have come from sick people. There is an ongoing police inquiry into these. The only solution to this kind of thing is to get the imbeciles caught. Initially, we sifted through the mail and removed offensive letters. I know staff at our training ground vetted my post and attempted to keep the worst examples away from me. But eventually we had to call in the police. The threats to my family and me were too serious, and we couldn't afford to take any chances.

Unfortunately, there was a racist element to some of the hate mail. Certain misguided Asians apparently wanted to declare a *jihad*, a holy war, on the players because of the charges they faced. It was also the case that Lee Bowyer received more personal abuse, in the shape of both vicious letters and taunts from opposition fans, than anyone else involved in the trial. Perhaps his profile was higher at certain points of the season. Whatever the reason, on the pitch he had to cope with many more vocal insults than Jonathan Woodgate did.

It did concern me that the West Yorkshire police, called in to investigate the hate mail, were from the same team that had investigated Bowyer and Woodgate and provided the prosecuting evidence for the trial. I didn't feel that they took the letters very seriously at first. They didn't seem to be worried about my family, and gave me no feedback on the progress of their inquiries or advice on security issues. In the end I requested a meeting with them and asked whether it would be better to invite a different force to look into my complaints as it seemed possible that there was a fundamental conflict of interests between the two investigations. On one hand they were working towards a conviction against two Leeds United players, while on the other they were being required to supervise the security of another Leeds United employee. After that I was offered

round-the-clock protection and a few ideas for security measures that helped the club to ensure my safety and the wellbeing
of my family.

It seemed to me that Woody's agents, Sfx, guided by Tony
Stephens, were intent on conducting their own separate campaign on behalf of their client and on distancing him from the
club. During the countdown to the trial they wanted to know
about everything that was going on at the club but reciprocated
with information on a need-to-know basis. Bowyer, Hackworth
and Duberry, meanwhile, ended up with one London-based
legal team with the blessing of the club.

I arranged meetings with the players' parents, who were
shocked when they realised the potential penalties available to
the court if the charges against the boys were proven. A spell in
prison, perhaps for a long time, was mandatory for the serious
assault charge. We were not talking about suspended sentences
or community service orders. That hit home with the families,
particular Bow's, as he had a previous conviction as a youngster
that was likely to increase any punishment he might face if
found guilty this time.

The atmosphere in the meetings I had with the players was
tense, but they did encourage Bow and Duberry to open up a
little. In fact, Michael was quite candid in a discussion we had
on the forecourt of the training ground one morning. He told
me that he had done nothing wrong, and shouldn't have been in
the predicament he was, but he had been guided in a direction
he wasn't happy about. He had, he said, been advised to stick to
a story that was getting him into trouble. He knew there was
only one way to deal with the situation and that was to tell the
truth. He eventually explained this to the court, though his
lawyer vehemently denied giving him such advice.

However, I sensed that Woody was telling us only what he
had to. There were perhaps two reasons for this. First, I suppose
he was protecting his Middlesbrough friends – some of whom,

it was claimed in court, had sparked the confrontation outside the Majestyk Nightclub. I had been hearing that he wasn't mixing with the right company and had been concerned about this for quite a while. As a well-known footballer, sometimes you have to accept that your life has changed and turn away from some of the lads you once knocked around with if they are the sort that might get you into trouble. Because if they do, it will be you who finishes up on the front pages of the national newspapers, not your friends. It is one of the prices you pay for acquiring the fame and fortune of a professional sportsman. Secondly, Tony Stephens' crew seemed keen to create the impression that because their client was tied to Sfx and Leeds United had nothing to do with his defence, he was going to get off. I always had the feeling that Woody was holding back; that he had another agenda.

The meetings with the accused players eventually petered out. We were still getting reports from our private detective, but by now the case was too far advanced for us to do anything more. Now we had to leave it in the hands of the police and the defence solicitors.

It is my sincere opinion that Woody, Bow, Hackworth and Dubes are decent boys and that they did not go out that night looking for aggro. I have never seen in any of them any suggestion that this kind of behaviour was likely.

Since the incident Lee has matured an awful lot. He has grown up and become a better person. During one of our meetings before the trial, he actually said to me: 'Boss, I know I'm not going to enjoy this, but if there is justice in this world, I will be found innocent.' I believed him. As for Woody, just before the trial began I spoke to his agent after a match at Aston Villa. Tony Stephens told me that they had a wonderful legal team, a wonderful case and that Woody would have no problems. I told him I hoped he would be proved right.

What made these terrible events and the timing of them even

worse was that there could be no doubting the astonishing potential of these footballers. I am Woody's greatest admirer as well as his sharpest critic. He can be awesome as a centre back. He could be the England centre back for the next decade alongside his clubmate Rio Ferdinand. He's outstanding on the ball, quick and good in the air. He reads the game well and is intelligent on the field. There is still room for improvement, though. He has to concentrate more and erase the sloppiness from his game and needs to display a more serious approach to training, to stop thinking of training as a laugh. He must take every game as his chance to prove that he is the best player in England. I think he finds that difficult.

I hope that when his career is over he will look back and realise why I have been hard on him at times. He has the ability to be a truly great player, but if he doesn't learn these lessons, though he might look great to his mates now, he'll have let himself down and failed to fulfil his promise.

Michael Duberry, who maintained that if he had been advised to tell the whole story from the beginning he would not have been in any trouble, is a great lad, full of fun, and popular with all his team-mates. Everybody likes to be with him. I call him 'The Big Easy' out on the pitch. This big, likeable, easygoing lad does need to be a meaner centre half on the field. But if he heads the ball away and passes it as neatly as possible, he has the ability to be a top-quality, no-frills centre half at Leeds United.

3

Good Side, Bad Side?

I'm a stubborn sod who refuses to panic when things are going wrong. As the 2000–01 season got underway, it was just as well, after a four-goal Champions League mauling at the hands of Barcelona at the Nou Camp on 13 September, followed by a Premier League defeat against Ipswich, I sensed that a few people around the club were beginning to wobble. We'd lost a few games by this time and I decided we needed to look at the overall picture to stop the rot.

I don't want to keep invoking an image of myself as the young manager, but the fact remains that my career had been relatively brief. Even so, I was learning plenty of significant lessons along the way, and one of them was that I would have had a major problem if I had had the club's best firepower at my disposal for selection and we were still losing games. As it was, we were plagued by injuries, so we simply had to patch up the team, battle on and avoid any hint of alarm.

Steve McManaman was mentioned as a potential signing from Real Madrid, but I was put off that idea by the prospect of Harry Kewell's return from injury in the long term. Harry is one of the most exciting attacking talents in the country and a greater goalscoring threat than McManaman. I rate Steve very highly, but I didn't want to sign a high-profile player who might end up surplus to requirements once Harry was ready to resume raiding from the left flank with the freedom to roam into other areas.

Against Ipswich on the Saturday after the Barcelona debacle we looked shattered. Ipswich's winning goal came after a mistake by Stephen McPhail, who shouldn't even have been on the field that day – soon afterwards he was dispatched for the operation he required on his damaged Achilles' tendon. In the closing stages of that 2–1 home defeat, and after the final whistle, I could hear abuse coming from small sections of the Elland Road crowd. After what we had achieved over the previous couple of seasons, I felt that was a very harsh reaction. There were certainly some painfully short memories out there. We keep all the letters we receive on file and I can tell you that there are some folk who only write when they want to knock us. We only hear from them when things are going wrong, never when we're reaching the Champions League semi-finals.

I would love to have a supply of beacons I could place on each and every one of the boo-boys in our crowd. Then, in the good times, when everyone is cheering, I'd be able to look into the crowd and identify the ones who have shown little or no tolerance or support when we have really needed it. It's in the bad times that fans really show their true worth and loyalty, and 99 per cent of ours are magnificent. We couldn't ask for better. But that small minority can cause problems by turning on their team and undermining performances when we're having a difficult run.

There was a constant theme to the first half of the season, and that was our inconsistency. The injuries were an ongoing handicap and the principal single reason for our plight, so it became tiresome to be asked every week whether we could transfer our European form into the Premiership and make a serious assault on the summit of the top division. The game against Derby the next Saturday was a case in point. We travelled to Pride Park after a great result against Milan in midweek, having beaten Paolo Maldini and his mates 1–0 to enhance our chances of qualifying from the first stage of the Champions League. We looked a bit tired but I couldn't freshen the team up – I had no options. After taking the lead through Ian Harte we played poorly in the second half, and gave away a sloppy equaliser to Derby's Georgian star, Georgi Kinkladze. I suppose the 1–1 scoreline was a fair result, but it wasn't good enough. We needed to win at places like Pride Park to emphasise our growing status in the game. The loss of Michael Duberry, who collapsed in that match having severed his Achilles' tendon, was typical of the misfortune that dogged us. Michael was probably playing as well as at any time in his career (I'll never forget his marking of Milan's Andriy Shevchenko four days earlier – he never gave him a kick), so the injury to him was a massive blow.

I'd had a right go at Michael after a pre-season game at Huddersfield some weeks earlier, a real heart-to-heart. As he sat in the corner of the dressing room I got down on my knees, looked him squarely in the eye and I told him what I expected of a centre half in my team. I said he was a smashing lad but that I thought he was too easygoing. He was developing into the club comedian, looking to have a laugh at everything, and I didn't want that. Look at the size of him, and he has pace and he's good in the air. He needed to make more of his natural ability.

Eddie Gray, my assistant manager, said he felt embarrassed for Dubes, but I felt it was something that had to be said. I wanted a reaction – I just hoped it would be the right reaction.

That day I put Alan Smith right on a few issues as well. I didn't speak to him in the dressing room. As he was a youngster, I thought he would handle it better if I talked to him away from the others, so we walked out on the pitch after the stadium had emptied. I didn't feel his approach had been right in that friendly game, and I told him a few home truths. I got a great response from both Michael and Alan. There was no sulking or refusing to speak to me. They were both determined to go out and show me what they could do for the team. It was the perfect reply. That way they could meet my eye in the knowledge that they had addressed my concerns brilliantly.

I remember blanking managers who had been critical of me when I was a player myself. I realise now the futility of that strategy. As a manager you have so many pressing matters to deal with that when you go home at night nothing could be further from your mind than the player who didn't acknowledge your 'good morning' at the start of the day.

The week after the Derby game, Mark Viduka arrived back from Olympic duty. Given our injury problems we could have done with him not having gone at all, but he had always been open about his intentions. He had made it clear when he agreed to join us that he was committed to appearing for the Socceroos, and we could hardly complain about him wanting to represent his country, especially since the football tournament was being staged in his home city of Melbourne. I did feel that once Australia had been eliminated he could have got back a couple of days earlier, perhaps even in time to take part in the Derby match, but there was no big fall-out. I just called Mark into my office, told him I was a bit disappointed by that and then pitched him back into the side for the Champions League game against Besiktas. Having failed to score a goal for us in his opening five appearances, he soon put that right in the 6–0 thrashing of the Turks, and then went on to become our leading goalscorer.

Good Side, Bad Side?

Attempting to reduce the fatigue induced by travelling in Europe before big Premiership games was a problem we faced all season. I must praise chairman Peter Ridsdale for sanctioning the use of a Swiss company called PrivatAir which provided luxury planes with spacious accommodation and excellent service. Booking the cheapest charters can be a false economy, as one of our rival clubs discovered to their cost when they lost a top player for a couple of key games to a back injury caused by sitting in cramped conditions on a plane. We tried to ensure that the players were looked after, and that any medical care or treatment they needed could be accommodated. After taking on Besiktas in Istanbul we kept the players in Turkey overnight and then on the Thursday teatime flew straight to Manchester, where we were to play on the Saturday morning, to attempt to keep their energy levels high. But the loss of Michael Bridges for the rest of the season with a serious ankle injury, plus knocks to Danny Mills and Eirik Bakke, left us reeling.

In fact we found ourselves heading for a showdown with Manchester United at Old Trafford with an entire eleven-man line-up of star players absent through injury. The team of missing men read: Martyn; Mills, Radebe, Duberry, Harte; Bakke, Dacourt, Batty, Wilcox; Kewell and Bridges. Even United boss Sir Alex Ferguson was forced to sympathise with our dire situation before the kick-off.

However, we didn't do too badly in the first half, and even had a couple of chances to score before the home side took the lead with a debatable goal just before the interval. Unfortunately, though, we were well and truly beaten in the second half, eventually losing 3–0. You need your full crew as badly at Old Trafford as you do at the Nou Camp. With the kind of injury problems we had at the time, all you can do is battle for all you are worth and hope that your fighting spirit will help you pull off a good result.

There has been a massive debate in English football about the impact of European competition on domestic performances. Our experience at Leeds has convinced me that if we are to do our best in Europe and then produce our best in the Premiership, we must be allowed extra rest periods between games. For instance, I don't think teams playing in Europe on a Wednesday night should be expected to play in the Premiership until the following Sunday.

We did get the occasional lucky break along our Premier League route. I still cannot fathom how we managed to beat Liverpool 4–3 at Elland Road on 4 November before our vital trip to play AC Milan in the San Siro. Suffice it to say we were indebted to Mark Viduka for his four-goal heroics that day. When Liverpool, with all their big guns available, went two goals up I was convinced we were going to take a pasting. I read on the day of the game that Liverpool manager Gérard Houllier had said he couldn't understand why we were making so much of our injury situation, which I found bizarre: our squad was so decimated that I didn't even have enough players to name five substitutes on our bench.

In the early exchanges Jonathan Woodgate pulled up with an injury and had to come off as we were conceding those two scores. I didn't think Liverpool were playing brilliantly, but our defending was poor, and we gave those goals away cheaply. At the other end, though, Viduka and Alan Smith always looked a handful for the visitors' defence, and you could see that we had the potential to score. We won, as I say, because of Viduka's brilliance in tucking away four superb strikes of different types. His eye for goal was deadly. I've never seen Gérard Houllier so down after a game in his life. He was virtually speechless. He didn't know how his team had been beaten.

After his fourth goal, Mark looked across to the dugout and crossed himself. I did the same. It was the first time in my life I had done that during a game, but it was no big issue, just a response to Mark. I remember telling Mark that day that my

mother had always liked him, but that when she saw him crossing himself on the field she thought he was an even nicer lad. Not
everybody agreed. His gesture provoked outrage among a small
number of supporters in the loyalist areas of Belfast. Those who
wrote to the club to complain were told that we sign players irre-
spective of their colour or their creed.

When the match was over Liverpool's Gary McAllister made
a comment to Eddie Gray that suggested he had not expected to
see a Leeds player blessing himself these days, and when we visited Anfield the next April, he asked my coach, Roy Aitken,
whether I was still crossing myself. Gary is a good lad, a great
professional, and I was pleased that he enjoyed such a great
season with Liverpool, playing a key role in their unique treble
of UEFA Cup, FA Cup and League Cup. I realise that people
can be sensitive, but I must say I was surprised that he seemed
to have allowed something like this to upset him over all those
months.

After a 1–1 draw in Milan ensured our place in the second
phase of the Champions League, we headed to Chelsea for a
Sunday afternoon game. You could see that the players had
benefited from the extra day's rest; in fact, the performance at
Stamford Bridge was one of our best of the season thus far. We
were controlled and powerful, we retained possession well and
you could feel the confidence improving throughout the squad.
The only thing that took the shine off it was coming away with
only one point for a 1–1 draw. We felt we deserved more than
that.

The Stamford Bridge match provided Jimmy Floyd
Hasselbaink with the chance to remind the club that had sold
him to Atlético Madrid sixteen months earlier of his talents.
Here he was back in the Premiership and doing well for Chelsea,
ready to prove a point or two. Indeed, the Sunday papers had
been full of his predictions as to what he was going to do with
us. I asked Lucas Radebe to mark Jimmy, and he was all over

our former centre forward like a rash. Jimmy hardly had a kick.

There are times when you can spot a steely glint in Lucas's eyes as he goes about his defensive job with calm authority, and this was one of them. He wasn't prepared to give Jimmy so much as a sniff at our goal. Mark Viduka put us ahead and we looked to be cruising to a victory until Chelsea grabbed a late equaliser from a hotly disputed free kick. We drew some consolation from the words of Chelsea coach Claudio Ranieri in the post-match analysis. He accepted that we were the better team and pointed to the reputation we were gaining in Europe as one of the up-and-coming sides. His praise was nice to hear and appeared to be genuine.

It was reassuring to see Lucas in such commanding form because the injuries he had sustained during our campaign had compounded an ongoing chronic degenerative problem with his knee. It's a source of great sadness to me that he has been afflicted like this. Three or four years ago, he was as accomplished a central defender as you could find in the world, and a great man off the field, too. He's not as supreme an all-round player as Rio Ferdinand, in whom we were by then very interested. Rio is more composed on the ball and a better passer – but in terms of marking opponents, Lucas was as good as you could get. He defended by instinct. His captaincy of South Africa wasn't based on talking or on traditional styles of leadership: he led by example. He used to stagger me when he used to play for his country, fly home and then run out to play for Leeds just twenty-four hours after getting off the plane. Many top managers recognised his ability, and we could have sold him many times over. Liverpool were keen to sign him when George Graham left Leeds. Gérard Houllier has often joked that he would have lured Lucas away if I hadn't stayed on as George's successor.

We had Lucas examined by an orthopaedic consultant in the summer of 2000 and were warned that we would have to protect him from excessive wear and tear if he was to see out his career. He couldn't go chasing around the world to play for South Africa, jumping on and off planes here, there and everywhere with little time to rest between games, and in the close season, he must have a complete break. Lucas decided to take stock. He realised he had to protect his career. He was captain of Leeds, he had signed a new contract and he accepted that he had to be available for club commitments and not dashing off for internationals in the southern hemisphere, which are played to a different calendar from the European games.

South Africa kept picking Lucas even though they knew he had this persistent injury. In the end, a delegation from the South African FA, consisting of Molefi Oliphant, their president, Irvin Khoza, vice-president, and chief executive Danny Jordaan, called in to see us when they were passing through Europe. Lucas, a couple of the Leeds directors and I had a meeting with them in my office at the training ground, and from the start Lucas made it clear that he wanted his views to be respected by everyone present. He explained that he couldn't keep playing for both club and country, so he would be able to play for South Africa only when it didn't jeopardise his knee or his Leeds career. In the circumstances it was agreed that Lucas would pack in international football. A formal document to this effect was signed and it seemed that the situation had been satisfactorily dealt with.

So you can imagine our astonishment when, within a few hours, stories began to appear in the South African press about how SAFA had triumphed and forced Leeds United into a massive climbdown. It was claimed that Lucas would be putting country before club and had insisted on being allowed to play for South Africa. Somebody had given the media the most ludicrous misinterpretation of events. I have a signed agreement that confirms my understanding of them. But if the media leaks weren't puzzling enough, what happened next beggared belief.

Having spent three hours in a meeting working out peace in our time with Lucas and accepting the retirement of their captain from international combat, the South Africans started naming him in every squad they nominated – even for the most low-key friendlies. It was a total contradiction of what we had agreed.

In an ideal world I'd have loved Lucas to have been able to play for Leeds and South Africa. I am well aware of his status as a national icon in his homeland. The great Nelson Mandela himself, speaking at a luncheon on a visit to Leeds, described Lucas Radebe as his hero, and declared himself honoured to be in the same room as him. And when South Africans were asked in a national poll to vote for the man or woman who epitomised the spirit of their nation, Lucas came second only to Mandela.

Lucas has no greater admirer than me. I knew him when he was a nobody, and now that he has become a great ambassador for his country he hasn't changed. He is prepared to make many sacrifices for his country: surely South Africa owes it to Lucas in return to allow him to prolong his career by concentrating on club football and the employers who, after all, pay his wages?

Meanwhile, in the Premiership, just when things appeared to be on the up after our excellent showing at Stamford Bridge, we took on West Ham at Elland Road and lost 1–0 to a goal that was down to sheer bad defending. It was Nigel Winterburn who scored for West Ham, with a header. How many times does Nigel pop headers into the net? I was very unhappy about that. Rio Ferdinand was outstanding for the visitors, and everyone at Elland Road that day, our fans included, must have realised why we were so keen to sign him. It was Rio's last Premiership appearance for the London club: just over a week later he had joined us for £18 million.

We had beaten Liverpool, gone to Milan and Chelsea and produced solid away performances, and yet here we were slipping back into our inconsistent form. We just couldn't get any momentum going in the Premier League. Perhaps the high point of that autumn was beating Lazio 1–0 in the Olympic Stadium in December in a magnificent team display. But then we flew back from Rome to meet Southampton at the Dell for our farewell match at that famous old stadium. We were a shadow of the team that had played so well in Italy, and it ended in another 1–0 defeat. Southampton took their chance in a scrappy game and we missed ours. It was a real anticlimax after the midweek events in the Olympic Stadium. Southampton played exactly as we had expected them to, so I was surprised and disappointed to hear afterwards that Southampton manager Glenn Hoddle had been holding court about how he had out-witted us in a tactical battle. The truth is that on the day we beat ourselves with some sloppy play. It was as simple as that.

Our preparations had not been helped by the British weather on the day before the game. We had chartered a flight from Leeds to Southampton but gale-force winds in Yorkshire forced the closure of the airport. After being involved in that horrifying plane crash taking off from Stansted a few years ago – having climbed to 150 feet, the pilot had had to crash-land in a field when he realised that one of the engines was on fire – many of our players are understandably not the best flyers, and the lads didn't want to take any chances in those conditions by switching to Manchester. So we had to call up the team coach and travel south on a motorway network that seems to grow more and more clogged up every Friday. All these last-minute arrange-ments meant that instead of reaching Southampton by three o'clock we didn't arrive until seven.

Hold-ups are inevitable whatever mode of transport you choose, of course. A few weeks later I was offered a lift home in golfer Lee Westwood's helicopter after we attended the BBC's Sports Personality of the Year Awards. Lee's a smashing lad and I get on well with him and his manager, Chubby Chandler. I told him I'd rather stick with the plane I was booked on, and you can imagine the ribbing I took when my flight was delayed and I didn't get back until 4 pm the following afternoon. Lee had been home since 10.30 in the morning. I hate helicopters. I have flown in one once, but the experience with the propeller-driven plane at Stansted had put me off. I stick to jets now.

It was at this midway point of the campaign that chairman Peter Ridsdale was working on prising Robbie Keane out of Inter Milan. Robbie very definitely interested me. However, I had already bought several new players, and had only just spent £18 million on Rio Ferdinand, and I knew that the funds available were not limitless. When we'd been to the San Siro in November to play AC Milan in the Champions League, who should show up at our pre-match training session at the stadium but Robbie, who is a mate of our Irish lads. It was great that Robbie seemed keen to be around our camp. He was asking the likes of Gary Kelly and Ian Harte about life at Leeds, and in turn we were able to get an idea of how he was faring in Italy. Inter was not the easiest club to play for given the constant changes to their backroom staff. When Marcello Lippi, the coach who had signed Robbie, had stepped down, he had quickly realised that the new regime didn't see him as a first-team regular striker, and it was clear that he would not be averse to coming home.

I told Peter Ridsdale that Robbie would be a great addition given his age, ability and attitude to the game. He absolutely fitted the bill in terms of the players I wanted in my squad. The chairman set up a meeting with Inter officials and Robbie's agents, but I knew we had a problem. We were aware that Liverpool and Chelsea also wanted to sign Robbie, and that they were prepared to lodge cash offers for the player, and we couldn't match their cash in a full payment deal. I must admit that I did wonder what my chairman could possibly achieve when he met the Inter officials. But he duly pulled off a transfer coup by somehow persuading Inter to accept a £1 million initial payment to secure Robbie on loan for the rest of the season on the basis that we would pay a further £11 million in the summer. The fact that Robbie told the Inter hierarchy Leeds was his first-choice club undoubtedly helped to clinch the deal but even so, I was genuinely amazed that Peter Ridsdale pulled off that transfer given the extraordinarily uneven financial playing field on which he was competing.

Sometimes Peter can drive me mad, but I know I work for the best chairman in football, and at the start of the 2000–01 season I had signed a five-year deal. It was a contract Peter wanted to seal because he wanted continuity at Leeds for the playing and managerial staff. In some respects, though, it is actually a one-year roll-on, since the club would have to pay me only one year's salary if they decided to get rid of me.

There has been a lot of debate about managers' contracts and whether or not they are adequately honoured on either side. On one hand managers stand accused of walking out on jobs when ambition lures them elsewhere, but on the other the lack of loyalty displayed by most clubs encourages them to be opportunist in their attitude. Look at the situation at Tottenham when they wanted to get rid of George Graham. It was the worst-kept secret in football that Spurs were courting Glenn Hoddle to replace him, yet when they did get George out he had to fight for his contractual rights.

When two parties are blatantly disloyal, nobody gets any sympathy. My beliefs are clear cut. If a club wants to sack its manager, it should settle his contract in full, and nobody else should accept that job until the outgoing boss has received proper compensation. And if a manager signs a contract he should have to stay at a club and honour it. I think it would be a good idea to introduce a regulation to this effect, binding on both sides, with the only get-out an arrangement between two clubs agreeing a compensation package to buy out a manager's contract. If such a rule were brought in we might end up seeing these matters handled with some decency.

In December, the injury epidemic began to ease at last. In the middle of the month Sunderland visited Elland Road. The atmosphere at fixtures between our clubs is almost like that of a derby. The rivalry probably dates back to the 1973 FA Cup final, when Sunderland pulled off one of the biggest shocks in living memory by defeating Don Revie's great Leeds side. For this Sunderland visit I was able to name Harry Kewell in the starting line-up for the first time in the season, and David Batty, a long-term absentee with heel and heart-muscle injuries, was among our substitutes.

I admire Batts immensely. He had been blighted by injuries since his return to Leeds from Newcastle, but you cannot underestimate his experience and competitive spirit. On the eve of the campaign I had announced that David would be out for the season. He had suffered an horrific injury and I'd been told he would be sidelined for a year. I hoped we might get him back earlier, but publicly writing him off for the whole season took the pressure off him, prevented people from continually asking him when he would be back, and ensured that the Batty recovery programme was not a permanent issue in the media. I knew that our physiotherapist, Dave Hancock, and Batts had gelled well, and the medical team deserve credit for getting Batts back so soon. So does the player himself, for the positive attitude he displayed. He was a human dynamo, working away on his fitness from early in the morning until late in the evening. The well-deserved ovation that greeted him when he ran on to the field as a substitute against Sunderland was one of the most deafening receptions heard at Elland Road all season. The public of Leeds were delighted to see a son of Leeds returning to combat.

Kewell was not completely right after his Achilles' tendon operation, but I knew he could bring an extra attacking dimension to the team, an element of creative play and goalscoring that had been sorely missed in his absence. After two bad League defeats at Leicester and Sunderland I knew we had to get back into the winning habit, and Sunderland were enjoying a rich vein of form, so this was a tough match for us.

Being able to put Kewell's name on the teamsheet was a boost to me, too. Analysing the increased options open to me in terms of selection rekindled my confidence, and seeing players returning after lengthy lay-offs really lifted my spirits. I sensed we were finally getting back on track. We beat Sunderland 2–0 and thoroughly deserved the victory. I saw the shape of a real Leeds United side that day. Rio was bedding in at the back and gave a commanding performance against Niall Quinn. We had badly needed the encouragement of a good win, and now we had got it. Sunderland boss Peter Reid had a drink with me after the game. I enjoy his company: he tells you what he thinks, and has clear views on the game. I suppose he manages his club in much the same way as he used to play. He's a straightforward fellow, and I respect him for it.

Aston Villa visited us a week later, on 23 December, and just when I thought we had turned the corner and were ready to enjoy a revival, we let ourselves down again. It was galling. We gave a stupid goal away just before half-time to a Villa team that had become our bogey side and ended up losing 2–1. Our inability to string a run of victories together was becoming deeply frustrating. On Boxing Day we headed north to play Newcastle at St James's Park. The players reported for duty at four o'clock in the afternoon on Christmas Day. I could tell that some of the lads were still down after the Villa defeat.

After twenty-five years in football, I'm accustomed to spending Christmas away from home, but if ever I wished for a winter shutdown, it was this Christmas. If only we could have had a recess after the Aston Villa game and given the players a break. Instead we were left asking them for a big performance at Newcastle, and we played terribly. We took an undeserved lead through Olly Dacourt, but Newcastle fought back and beat us 2–1. Rio Ferdinand endured his worst game since he'd joined Leeds, while Harry Kewell took a whack on his Achilles' tendon and was forced out of the fray. He was to be absent for another seven weeks of this injury-ravaged season. Back at home that night there was a party awaiting me: because footballers are invariably absent on Christmas Day, Boxing Night tends to become a focal point for family celebrations. After losing at Newcastle, I needed that like a hole in the head. I just wasn't in the mood for it, but of course you have to make the effort.

I was away on New Year's Eve, too, as we prepared for the game against Middlesbrough on 1 January. Boro, with Terry Venables in charge, were predictably well organised. I warned my players that they must remain alert because I had an idea the visitors would play on the break and look to exploit any chance that came their way. We dominated proceedings at first; then, just before half-time they attacked, as anticipated, on the break. Alen Boksic caught our defence flat-footed and dispatched a great strike. It was everything we had talked about, but we still hadn't learned our lesson. However, we took control in the second half and grabbed an equaliser through substitute Robbie Keane. His first score for the club since his loan move from Inter Milan paved the way for a golden run of goals that were vital to our chances of revitalising our season.

Terry Venables is a master of manipulation in dealing with the media, so I shouldn't have been surprised when he went into the press room and announced that his team had been robbed. They'd had all of one shot on goal! In one sense a draw against relegation-threatened Middlesbrough wasn't a great result, but at least we had earned something from the game. A draw was better than many of our recent results.

We were thirteenth in the League at this juncture, and our next match was away to Manchester City, who were third from the bottom and, more pertinently, just six points behind us.

Defeat against City would plunge us nearer to the relegation zone, and give the Mancunians a massive lift and help to convince them that they could survive and drag us into the relegation dogfight. In short, victory was nothing less than critical. The awareness that we could slide into trouble if we screwed up at Maine Road permeated the club. I was worried whether such a young group of players would cope with the pressures of a relegation battle. We just had to make sure we didn't dally too close to the lower reaches. On the eve of the match I dared to mention the dreaded 'R' word at my press conference. Relegation was an issue lurking on the horizon and I felt the time had arrived for a few home truths.

On the morning of the game we heard the tragic news that coach Roy Aitken's father had died in Scotland. Roy left the team hotel to join his immediate family in Yorkshire before heading north to identify his dad. It was a painful demonstration that you must keep a sense of perspective in football. We all felt for Roy and his family.

The papers that Saturday were full of threats from Alfie Håland, a former Leeds player and now the City skipper, about what he was going to do to us and how we would be dragged into the relegation zone by City. Quite how former players allow themselves to be lured into slagging off their old mates I will never know, but Alfie certainly made my team talk easier. The lads went out and gave a very good performance, and we beat City 4–0. Robbie Keane came on as substitute again and grabbed a couple of late goals. Perhaps the scoreline flattered us a bit, but we deserved to win nonetheless. And crucially, we'd put daylight between us and the clubs about to be cut adrift at the bottom.

But just when it seemed we had turned another corner, we were plunged back into the depths by the following week's 3–1 home defeat against Newcastle United. It was after this setback that I felt a degree of panic was beginning to engulf Elland

Road. It was a backdrop I had to deal with. We produced a poor display against Newcastle, the only team to do the Double over us in the Premier League that season. Robbie Keane, who had scored three goals from the substitutes' bench, was handed his first place in the starting line-up and fired us into an early lead. But after that we never played. We slid back into our shells and were caught on the break like novices.

Joy and I were due to go out for dinner with Allan Leighton, vice-chairman of Leeds United plc, the football club's parent company, and his wife Annie that night. My son John was scheduled to spend a year working for Allan, who is a very successful businessman, and we were planning to discuss that. In the immediate aftermath of the Newcastle defeat I really didn't fancy fulfilling the fixture. I was in a bleak mood, and was going to cry off. But Peter Ridsdale told me that I should go, and he was right. Allan was great company, which is just what I needed, because I endured a very traumatic hour after the game.

I try to stay out of boardrooms. Things can be said there immediately after a game, while emotions are still running high, that can sting a manager into biting back. The directors may mean no harm, but it's a situation I prefer to avoid where possible. If the chairman wants me, he knows where I am.

There is one director at Leeds I've known for many years, and on that day his knowledge of Peter Ridsdale and me proved invaluable. He saw how concerned the chairman was and knew I needed to sit down with Peter. So I headed down to the coaches' room to see the chairman. On the way I stopped my friend on the stairs and asked him: 'Do they want me to go?'

He replied: 'That's the last thing the chairman wants to hear. You're here to stay.'

I talked to the chairman for a long time, and Peter aired his concerns: not so much about that day's game, as about the future. He made it clear that we all needed to stick together to make the club a success. I assured him that I was not wavering in my belief that we could turn Leeds into a winning team and maintain our development into one of the top clubs in England and Europe.

It was unfortunate that another of our directors chose that night to go for a meal at a popular restaurant in Leeds frequented by partisan followers of the club. I understand that one particular table of fans weren't too impressed by his presence and made their feelings clear. Apparently, at one stage a bread roll was thrown. There are times when you go out and mix with the fans, and times when it's in everyone's best interests to give people a little breathing space. Intentions and actions in the heat of the moment can be misunderstood. When I was told about the incident in the restaurant I have to say I wasn't surprised. Fans are passionate about their teams, and they felt hurt that day. So did I. Our own dinner with Allan and Annie Leighton was, thankfully, a quiet and discreet meal, and great therapy for me.

The next day I picked up the *Mail on Sunday* and read in Patrick Collins's column that he'd heard a caller ring a radio phone-in show calling for my sacking by Leeds. That was only to be expected. When radio stations have a phone-in they don't want to hear from the sane middle ground of supporters who recognise the problems a manager is dealing with and look at a bad game in the context of the progress their club has made. No, they want to hear from the extremists. It's the extremists who provoke a good argument. The only problem is that the views they put forward are often totally flawed and have on occasion been aired by fans of another club posing as a supporter of the team or manager they are criticising to make mischief with their local rivals. I rate Patrick Collins very highly – he is among the élite of our sportswriters and produces wonderfully written, witty columns as well as incisive interviews – so I was touched that he made it clear that, in his opinion, it would be an act of supreme folly if Leeds sacked me.

But articulate and supportive words from a great writer weren't the only things I needed for Leeds. I needed a few good victories to put some gloss on the domestic season.

Our trip to take on Tottenham, managed by my old mentor George Graham, on 24 February looked like a tough challenge. Part of the test for us was to show that this time we could return from a fantastic midweek journey in Europe, where we had beaten Anderlecht 4–1, reproducing in the Premier League the kind of form we had shown in the Champions League. I knew George would relish putting one over his old club and, despite the pressure building on his reign at White Hart Lane, Spurs had not in fact lost a home game all season.

We started marvellously well. Our confidence was still sky-high after our European victory and it came as a nasty surprise when Spurs took the lead against the run of play through Les Ferdinand. But we stuck to our principles, and goals from Lee Bowyer and an Ian Harte penalty clinched the match. George was honest in defeat, telling the post-match press conference that the best team had won and that the margin of victory could have been even greater. It was a marvellous three points for us, and the key to it all was having vital players like Harry Kewell, who had been badly missed earlier in the campaign, back in the fray – even if they weren't on peak form. With Lucas Radebe again becoming really troubled by his knee, Michael Duberry injured and Jonathan Woodgate unavailable because of the trial at Hull Crown Court, we turned to the defensive partnership of Rio Ferdinand and Dominic Matteo that was to lay the foundations of our spectacular run-in to the campaign. They blended together perfectly: both were willing to attack headers and had the pace and poise to pick up the pieces around their defensive colleagues. It may have been a defensive partnership forced on us by circumstances, but it proved impressive.

The members of the Leeds hierarchy who had been surprised by my team selection in the Champions League clash with Lazio needed to remember that I was looking beyond the meaningless stage-two game and towards a match I saw as critical to our movement up the Premiership League table: our trip to take on Charlton at the Valley on 17 March. Charlton were flying. They were enjoying a marvellous season and had been beaten at home only once. Manager Alan Curbishley has turned Charlton into a resolute team and their loyal followers create an intense atmosphere at their south-east London home. It seemed as if we were constantly travelling to face the form teams in the Premiership on their own soil. Spurs had been having a great run at home, now we were at the Valley and there was a visit to high-flying Sunderland in prospect later in the month.

I drafted Nigel Martyn, Olivier Dacourt, David Batty and Alan Smith back into the starting line-up and we got off to a flier against Charlton. Viduka curled in a deft opening goal within a couple of minutes which certainly deflated Charlton in the early exchanges, but we gifted them a stupid equaliser midway through the first half. Nigel Martyn, asked to leave his line and catch a speculative cross, allowed striker Shaun Bartlett to out-jump him and head into the vacant net. It was a sloppy way to allow the home side back into the game, and the match became physically tough as we attempted to take command again. It was Alan Smith who smashed home a fierce shot from the edge of the area in the second half to seal a hard-fought and important win from a very challenging game. Another great three points.

I didn't want us to lose momentum now that our League season had finally taken off and we were accumulating points at a much healthier rate, but the following weekend was designated for internationals, so we lost another posse of players and our training ground virtually closed down owing to international absences. It's at times like these that a club manager feels powerless to influence events around him. I headed off for a break in Dubai just hoping that I would get all my players back fit and ready to take on Sunderland at the Stadium of Light.

Unfortunately we did lose Dominic Matteo, but otherwise the team that had climbed from thirteenth place in early January to fifth on the morning of the Sunderland game, 31 March, was largely intact. Up to this point Peter Reid's side had lost only one home game all season. In my pre-match press conference I explained why I expected them to maintain their current form and claim a European qualification place. Twelve months earlier they had blown up in the run-in and lost their way, but they seemed to be in better nick all round this time. It was a huge test for us.

Reidy has made Sunderland into an ultra-competitive team who believe in the principles they play by, and I don't have a problem with that. The Stadium of Light is as good as any ground in the country and their supporters make it a marvellously noisy football theatre. This was one of the matches in which Rio Ferdinand won over his critics by playing quite brilliantly. He was without his regular partner at the back, Matteo, and in the early exchanges we also lost replacement centre back Lucas Radebe because of injury. We had to switch Danny Mills to central defence and bring Gary Kelly on at right back. Nevertheless Alan Smith put us ahead, and in the closing stages, when we had been reduced to ten men, Mark Viduka fired home to emphasise our superiority in a 2–0 victory. The one drawback was the sending-off of Smith for two bookable offences. I felt he was very harshly treated in being shown the red card.

It was on the morning of the Sunderland game that I heard the news of the death of the former Arsenal player David Rocastle at the age of only thirty-three. Rocky was a great friend of mine and I was truly shocked to learn that he had lost his battle against cancer. Rocky and I were, of course, from different generations at Arsenal – I was nine years his senior – but we shared the same birthday, 2 May. We had joined forces to celebrate Rocky's twenty-first and my thirtieth, taking our wives to

Dominic Matteo proved the bargain buy of the season at £3.75 million.

Andrew Varley Picture Agency

We had to wait a few weeks for Mark Viduka's first goal for Leeds, but when it came he celebrated it in style. He emerged as one of Europe's finest strikers during our Champions League adventure.

Andrew Varley Picture Agency

Danny Mills had taken time to settle, but he won over the fans with his up-and-at-'em approach.

Colorsport

Olly Dacourt could be impetuous in his tackling but he matured into a fine midfielder.

Andrew Varley Picture Agency

Lee Bowyer emerges through the media scrum at Hull Crown Court.

Popperfoto/Reuters

Bowyer and Woodgate appeared together on the football field as well as in the dock in Hull.

Colorsport

The first trial took its toll on Jonathan Woodgate, who lost weight at an alarming rate.

Popperfoto/Reuters

Bowyer's form in the Champions League was sensational. Here he revels in a match-winning performance against Anderlecht.

Popperfoto/Reuters

Lucas Radebe rises to the occasion but a chronic knee injury forced him to stand down from international duty with South Africa.

Colorsport

Robbie Keane, pictured with his new manager and chairman Peter Ridsdale, was wanted by Liverpool, Chelsea and Sunderland, but he chose Leeds and inspired our climb out of the lower reaches of the Premiership.

Empics Sports Photo Agency

The Manchester United goalkeeper, Fabien Barthez, walks away, but a penalty was awarded for his kick at Ian Harte.

Andrew Varley Picture Agency

Harte dusted himself down to take the spot-kick ... and missed.

Andrew Varley Picture Agency

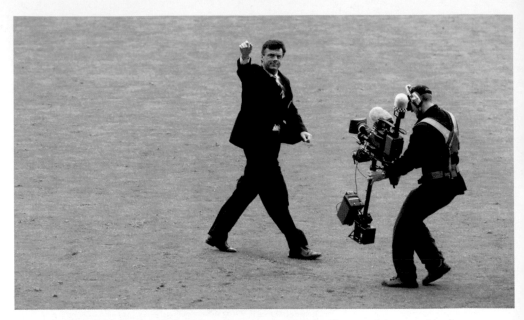

The loneliness of the long-distance manager. But on this occasion I am punching the air with joy.

Andrew Varley Picture Agency

Harry Kewell's return against Sunderland underlined the easing of our injury crisis.

Colorsport

see Luther Vandross in concert at Wembley Arena. I insisted we shared a bottle of champagne in a hotel close to the Arena beforehand. From then on Rocky maintained that I was the man who had introduced him to champagne. We had a lovely evening that will be a lasting memory for me of a great footballer and a wonderful man.

The following Friday I attended Rocky's funeral. It was a sad day for all of us who had seen the bright-eyed London boy grow up and become a star at Arsenal. David's daughter stood up at the service and said a few words. 'Dad, you're the best. We love you and we'll miss you.' I couldn't get those words out of my mind as I travelled north on the train that afternoon and they stayed with me that evening when I went out with my wife and children. That Rocky was as nice a man as you could wish to meet, a fantastic lad, shone through at the funeral. Everyone he'd ever come into contact with appeared to be there. It was a fitting testimony to one of the most popular footballers I have ever known. Leeds had beaten Deportivo La Coruña 3–0 in the Champions League a couple of days earlier, and old football friends came over to congratulate me on our success. But that victory paled into insignificance alongside the passing of David Rocastle and the pain his family were going through. It was another event in our rollercoaster season that put football in its true perspective.

If our performance in the destruction of Deportivo La Coruña at Elland Road stands out as the epic home display of the campaign, the way we played in the first half at Liverpool on Good Friday must rank alongside it in terms of away matches. We faced two monumental games in the space of four days over Easter: Liverpool were followed on the Tuesday by the second leg against Deportivo in Spain. But we could not afford to let our attention be distracted by that because we knew at this stage, in mid-April, that for the second season running it looked as if there was going to be a direct battle between us and

Liverpool for third place and the final Champions League qual-
ification berth. The alternative for us was to win the European
Cup and qualify automatically, but third place in the
Premiership was the more likely route.

We had an early kick-off at Anfield and in the first half we
probably played as well as we've ever played during my managerial reign. We scored twice, through Rio Ferdinand and Lee
Bowyer, and might have had more goals: Rio was getting a real
taste for them, to the extent that whenever we won a corner, our
fans would chant his name in the belief that he was sure to get
on the end of Ian Harte's crosses. We won the game in those
forty-five minutes. The overall performance of everyone, from
goalkeeper to the strikers, was absolutely top class. And we were
playing a quality side, with all their big guns in action. I was
proud of the way we dictated play and the whole tempo of the
match before half-time.

We gave a silly goal away to Michael Owen early in the second
half, and that inevitably put us under pressure. Our belief in the
way we play was tested, but we held firm and near the end Mark
Viduka was denied a third goal by a linesman flagging for offside
(replays showed the decision to have been wrong). The only
sour note was the dismissal of Liverpool's outstanding young
midfielder Steven Gerrard for a second bookable offence. It was
a very harsh decision. In fact our lads, led by David Batty, cam-
paigned to keep Gerrard on the pitch, but their protests were to
no avail. As vital as the three points our 2–1 victory brought us
were the three denied to our arch-rivals Liverpool. Yet although
this was a significant triumph, I knew it did not guarantee us
anything. The competition for the Champions League places
from Manchester United and Arsenal would be tight, and with
five games remaining, we had to maintain this kind of irresistible
momentum for the rest of the Premiership campaign with the
added bonus of anything Europe had to offer. These were heady
days.

Good Side, Bad Side?

The following Monday, on the eve of our quarter-final second-leg tie in La Coruña, I took a call in our team hotel from Gérard Houllier. The Liverpool boss chewed over our Friday game, wished me luck in the Champions League and said he was enjoying the countdown to the Mersey derby kick-off that Easter Monday evening. I wished him all the best, but told him I hoped his team got stuffed. Going down to reception in the lift later I heard that the score at Anfield seconds from the end was 2–2. A draw would have suited us fine, but by the time I got out of the lift, Liverpool had grabbed a late winner from Gary McAllister's free kick. It was a body blow to us. We would not feel the full ramifications of that goal until a few weeks later, but I have no doubt it was what inspired Liverpool's spectacular run-in. Their League season turned on that strike.

With our passage to the Champions League secured in mid-week, we headed to West Ham for another tough away game. The secret at this stage of the season is to try to keep your players as fit and fresh as possible. Unfortunately, on the day of the game we lost Mark Viduka with a tight hamstring so Robbie Keane came in as his replacement. It was Rio Ferdinand's first return to Upton Park, and it was refreshing to see him receiving a wonderful, warm welcome home from the West Ham fans. That doesn't happen too often these days when a former star returns to his old stamping ground, and I must admit I was astonished by it. I think Rio conducted himself very well in terms of explaining what West Ham meant to him and why he moved on.

You might say that Rio pushed his luck a bit, too, by scoring our second goal in a 2–0 win. The lad didn't have the heart to celebrate his third goal in just five games for us in front of the Hammers fans. While his new team-mates surrounded him and offered their salutes, Rio just kept his head down and marched back for the kick-off. The West Ham supporters realised at that moment how much their club still meant to its former son.

We had another controversial sending-off in this game when David Batty was red-carded for a challenge on Joe Cole. Referee Graham Poll was convinced that Batts had elbowed Cole in the face, but from my position in the dugout it did not appear that there had been any contact, and Batts maintained that he had not touched Cole. However, I have to concede that the referee got it right. While one camera angle failed to offer any great insight, another showed exactly what happened. I don't think David was being malicious. He braced himself and went into a tackle, and unfortunately, his forearm clipped Joe's face. It was not a full-blooded or premeditated smash to the face. In the closing stages West Ham were able to make more of a game of it with only ten men to deal with, but we held out for our victory. The more serious consequence was that we would now lose Batty for the last three League games of the season.

We were now up in fourth position in the Premiership with our sights set on overhauling Liverpool and claiming that Champions League place. Considering where we had been in December and early January, it was a spectacular revival. In fact, since the turn of the year we had been accumulating points at a faster rate than any other team in the English top flight. We had a clear week to prepare for the visit of Chelsea to Elland Road, which had now taken on a special significance: a win would guarantee us a berth in the UEFA Cup next season. It would also mean we wouldn't have to spend the summer taking part in the Intertoto Cup, for which we had been entered by the club in a decision with which I was not entirely happy. I felt that even if we missed out on Europe, we might be better off spending the summer licking our wounds, resting some very tired players and preparing for a real tilt at success in the 2001–02 season.

So it was a must-win game, and Chelsea had been enjoying a rich seam of form. I avoided getting involved in the clamour about Jimmy Floyd Hasselbaink's return to Elland Road. Jimmy is a class finisher and would score goals in any team, but I didn't want to be linked to the kind of debate about the return of a former hero that so often degenerates into a slanging match. It was a tight game and in the second half, with the match goalless, I sent on Robbie Keane as a substitute for Harry Kewell, pushing him into attack alongside Viduka and Smith. It took us a good while to wear them down, but Robbie broke the deadlock and then, late on, Viduka smashed a ferocious shot into the top corner for our second goal in a 2–0 victory. European competition for the next season had been secured.

This success epitomised the experience we had gained from playing in Europe and the patience that was developing in the side. We had learned how to handle tight situations and how to win games. We had realised that we couldn't always steamroller teams into submission, and that there were times when you had to display gritty resolve to grind out a favourable result. Increasingly, we were scoring crucial goals late in matches. A very young Leeds United team was growing up, and our new coach, Brian Kidd, played his part in this new maturity. He had experienced a similar development with Manchester United and I think that knowledge earned him special respect in our dressing room.

With the UEFA Cup place assured, we pursued our ultimate goal: qualification for the Champions League in 2001–02. The last major League test we faced was the trip to my old Highbury headquarters on 5 May. The match fell between the Champions League semi-finals against Valencia, and a rumour spread through football that I was going to deliberately field a weakened team in north London to protect my players after the first of those games, a goalless draw at home to Valencia. I wish life were as simple as that. I did face a selection quandary, and I would have loved to have been able to rest a few of my key men after the series of tough games we'd faced. I knew the match at Highbury would be physical and bruising, but we still had to send out our best team. We couldn't afford to take it easier in the domestic game because a positive result was so critical to us. We had to run the risk of losing players we couldn't replace.

The combative David Batty was already absent through suspension, and the programme of demanding fixtures we'd endured over a number of weeks suddenly took its toll. We were well beaten, 2–1, by a quality Arsenal side; we should have been annihilated in the first half. It was our worst away performance of the season. I think some of the lads had the second leg of the Champions League semi-final on their minds. To them it was a case of let's go to London, play the game and get out of town without too many bumps and bruises. I was very disappointed.

In one way the final week of the Premiership season, which involved home games against Bradford City and Leicester City, could not have been better planned. On the downside, though, we faced the horrible possibility that a sense of total anticlimax might engulf the club and we might see the season end with a whimper rather than a bang. The League defeat against Arsenal was followed by our exit from the Champions League against Valencia, just one step away from the final. I was determined not to allow these body blows to undermine everything we were working towards.

My target was to collect six points from the final two games. Nothing less would do. On the Friday night before our Sunday night meeting with Bradford, I travelled to the San Siro Stadium to watch the Milan derby. That fabulous football theatre was, of course, the venue for the Champions League final and brought back happy memories of our previous visit there. I couldn't help wonder what life might have been like if we'd qualified to face Bayern Munich in Europe's biggest game. AC whacked Inter 6–0 that night, and I witnessed an impressive refereeing display by the Italian Pierluigi Collina, the best ref in the business.

I watched the FA Cup final the next day at Cardiff and saw Arsenal batter Liverpool for 86 of the 90 minutes, only to lose the game. That's cup football for you. Given my long service at Highbury I was sorry for the Gunners but as a friend of Gérard Houllier's, I was delighted for him. He had guided Liverpool to a treble of trophies – a remarkable achievement.

As we went into the Bradford game the next day, I told the players there had to be absolutely no suggestion that they were feeling sorry for themselves. We were now laying down the ground rules for next season, and I wanted them to show everybody that they could cope with adversity and disappointment, bounce back with tenacity and prove they were all winners, individually and collectively. There was no doubting their response: we ran all over Bradford, thrashing them 6–1 – a great result for a local derby. We were also treated to the unedifying spectacle of two Bradford players fighting each other. It was unbelievable, and I was glad it wasn't something I had to deal with. All six goals came from different players, which was a remarkable feat in itself. I think we pleased our fans with the way we disposed of our local rivals. It was a thoroughly professional performance.

As our last game, against Leicester, approached, the Champions League qualification issue was going right to the wire. If Liverpool won at Charlton, they were through; if they drew and we could beat Leicester, we'd be through. If you ask me to say totally honestly what I thought would happen, it was that Liverpool would make it. There was a sense of déjà vu to proceedings, because we'd pipped them on the final day of the season twelve months earlier. On that occasion we had travelled to London to play West Ham while Liverpool were competing in Yorkshire against relegation-threatened Bradford City. This time we were in Yorkshire, at Elland Road, and they were in London, south of the River Thames at the Valley. I couldn't see it happening again, especially as Liverpool had responded so well after we defeated them at Anfield on Good Friday. After that setback we knew Gérard Houllier's team would be keen to prove their point. It was a tall order for them, but I felt things were going their way. They had a great squad of players with an array of really potent attacking options. Gérard could rest Michael Owen and opt for a partnership of Robbie Fowler and Emile Heskey, or interchange the trio. And indeed they met our challenge in some style.

Liverpool were hammered in the first half at the Valley and it looked as if they might be left crying into their glasses again. At Elland Road we had to be patient in breaking down Leicester's massed defence, but we ran out worthy 3–1 winners. Unfortunately for us, down the road in south-east London, Liverpool got a grip in the second half and finally emerged with an emphatic 4–0 victory. I telephoned Gérard that evening to congratulate him, and in the background I could hear the noise of euphoric Liverpool players celebrating on the team coach. It was a complete role reversal from twelve months earlier. I could imagine how they were feeling.

We all need luck in life, and Liverpool enjoyed their fair share of it in the run-in to their historic treble campaign. I don't begrudge it one bit. I just hope Leeds can enjoy the same degree of good fortune in the future. It makes the vital difference between getting close to trophies and actually winning them.

4

Unrated and Into Europe

I am often asked to select my favourite moment or greatest triumph from our glorious 2000–01 European campaign. There are plenty to choose from, but in many ways there was no finer achievement than actually reaching the Champions League in the first place by overcoming Munich 1860, the fourth-best team in Germany, over two legs – especially at a time when our playing resources were stretched to breaking point.

In the Champions League qualifying rounds, the assumption is that clubs from the seeded nations will draw one of the weaker teams for a match that will be no more than a formality in admitting them to the competition proper. So what happened when Leeds were in the qualifying games? Instead of a Finnish side or the Estonian entrant, we drew Munich 1860 for a clash that made the seeding system appear irrelevant, and I met a man who would have few challengers as the most arrogant coach in Europe.

The fact that the first leg was at Elland Road before the start of our domestic Premier League offensive only made qualification harder. Talk about creating a tough pre-season programme: it couldn't have been any tougher than this.

Our pre-season preparations were a nightmare from day one. Harry Kewell, who had been suffering from that Achilles' tendon problem at the end of the previous campaign and had been advised to rest the injury, reported back, but on the third day of light training our physiotherapist, Dave Swift, told me that he might need more rest. I was shocked. After all, Harry had just had almost two months off. If anything needed doing with that tendon injury, I felt it should have been done during the close season. Jason Wilcox had undergone a knee operation and Stephen McPhail was also complaining of an Achilles' tendon problem. It seemed that a lot of medical complaints that ought to have been sorted out in the summer were all rearing their ugly heads together. The news that David Batty might be out for the season because of his Achilles' injury put the tin lid on it. It was unfortunate, but I felt that what was happening around the treatment room just wasn't right, and there was a parting of the ways with Dave Swift.

My first choice to replace him was Dave Fevre from Blackburn Rovers. Blackburn manager Graeme Souness gave me permission to speak to Dave, and initially he agreed to take the job, but because of family complications changed his mind and decided to stay at Ewood Park. I asked Dave who he would recommend, and he suggested another Dave – Dave Hancock, who worked for Fevre in the Blackburn Youth Academy. We got Hancock in, explained why his predecessor had gone and made it clear what we wanted from him. It was a tall order: he was inheriting a difficult task and had a monumental number of players to get fit, but he rose to the challenge and has done a great job for us.

So that was the injury-induced chaos enveloping the club as

we prepared for the significant task of trying to qualify for the Champions League proper. Mark Viduka wasn't fully fit for the first leg against Munich, but we had to wheel him out to play. The match was wrecked by the worst display of refereeing I've ever seen in my life. Never, as a player or a manager, have I witnessed the total incompetence displayed by Costas Kapitanis, the Cypriot official. The UEFA observer at the game recognised that he just wasn't good enough; I felt he was appalling, totally out of his depth. Amid a welter of yellow and red cards he sent off Eirik Bakke and Olivier Dacourt of Leeds as well as Munich's Ned Zelic.

The bald facts of the match are that we won 2–1. We were cruising with a two-goal lead but three minutes into injury time Thomas Hassler, the former Germany international who remains an outstanding creative talent in these latter days of his career, delivered a pinpoint cross. Lucas Radebe was outjumped and Paul Agostino buried a header past Nigel Martyn. I was well aware that the away goal could prove a savage blow before the Munich players left the field punching the air and doing high fives, confident that they would ease their way past us in the second leg at the Olympic Stadium. Their coach, Werner Lorant, said afterwards: 'That goal made a huge difference. If I had been offered a 2–1 scoreline beforehand I would have been quite happy with that, because I'm sure we'll do the business now in Munich.'

Alan Smith had put us ahead after thirty-nine minutes with his first goal since the FA Cup destruction of Manchester City the previous January. Viduka, making his competitive debut following his £6 million move from Celtic, won a battle for possession and pressurised Martin Stranzl into an unwise header towards his own goal. Munich keeper Michael Hoffman raced from his line but Smithy had anticipated the situation, and he reached the ball first and headed home. Our young striker was then tripped by Harald Cerny to earn Leeds a penalty in the seventy-first minute. It was successfully converted by Ian Harte, the first of the eleven goals he was to notch up for us in a memorable campaign. I can't think of another fullback in the world game to rival Hartey's goalscoring prowess. Roberto Carlos, the great Brazilian at Real Madrid, may dispatch the occasional wonder goal, but even he is not as prolific as our laid-back Irishman.

The exclusion of the suspended Bakke and Dacourt for the second leg, allied to our crippling list of unavailable, injured players, left me with massive selection problems as I attempted to patch up our side to produce a decent, competitive unit. Peter Ridsdale had come in to see me in the coaches' room after the first leg, delighted that we had established a lead, but all I could ask him was: 'Who should we send out to play in the second game? We're running out of players.'

I sat in my hotel room in Munich pondering the team I could field. The suspension of the two midfielders left us woefully depleted in that department. I had to nominate Gary Kelly, a right back, on the right side of midfield. Lucas Radebe, a central defender, was switched to a central midfield role. Matthew Jones, a home-grown youngster who moved on to Leicester City a few weeks later, was also in the centre, while Lee Bowyer, the only recognised first-team midfielder on the park, had to operate in an unaccustomed role on the left.

With our full team available we would have beaten Munich 1860 without too many problems. It is doing as well as we did in the absence of so many key personnel that makes this match one of the most satisfying we played in Europe. The patched-up team rolled their sleeves up and did brilliantly. The Olympic Stadium was a beautiful setting for a Champions League qualifier. We took a battering at times but in fact we wasted the best chance of the first half when Viduka intercepted a weak back pass and then fluffed his chance to beat Hofmann. As I walked along the running track at the start of the second half, there was a lovely interplay between Viduka and Smith, and the young striker held off two German defenders before slotting home a great goal. It was a significant moment for Leeds and for our goalscorer. He was to go on from here to create problems for some of Europe's finest defenders and most organised defences.

We had a few escapes, notably when the wily veteran Hassler struck a shot against the post. There was some good defending from centre backs Jonathan Woodgate and Michael Duberry, a couple of fine saves by Nigel Martyn and an athletic goal-line clearance from Danny Mills, but we held on to our 1–0 advantage that night to go through 3–1 on aggregate. We were in the Champions League.

There was one disappointment, though, on that warm August night in Bavaria, and that was how sour Werner Lorant, the Munich coach, was afterwards. I suppose I should have realised that he could be a touch idiosyncratic when I discovered he had performed a bungee jump for a television crew for a film shown to fans at half-time during one game. I spoke to him before our second leg match, shook his hand and wished him well. We both knew the stakes were huge for our clubs. Finances in football are vital these days, so we weren't playing just for honour and international pride. The prize of competing in Europe's premier club tournament with the élite clubs was within reach for one of our clubs, and I suppose it would be fair to say that the winners would be laughing all the way to the bank. Even so, you don't expect such behaviour from a top-level coach, let alone a fifty-one-year-old with such a wealth of experience – he was the man who had guided Munich 1860 back into Europe from the depths of Germany's regional league system.

After the match Lorant completely blanked me. He refused even to shake my hand, never mind speak to me. I told the press at the post-match conference that I hoped when I lose a game I show a bit more dignity than the sourpuss here. I would have loved to have played them again and given them a real thrashing.

Lorant seemed to think we were impostors in the competition, there only to make up the numbers, and I was angered by his arrogant attitude.

During the previous couple of seasons we had played against teams coached by some of the world's finest managers and tacticians, men like Fabio Capello at Roma who accepted defeat with good grace. Nevio Scala, the Italian who transformed the fortunes of Parma before heading to Besiktas of Turkey, saw his Turkish team suffer a 6–0 beating at Elland Road, but he didn't quibble. He looked me in the eye as he shook my hand and wished me good luck. Any team can lose, but you can lose in the right way. Those men had class.

We were only third seeds when the draw for the first stages of the Champions League was made, so we knew we would be paired with one other against two top-quality clubs. But nobody had dared to wonder whether the two in question might be AC Milan and Barcelona. It was a stunning group to be in. Without a doubt I would cite those two among perhaps four or five continental sides that must be considered the very élite of the European game. They boast massive followings and play in two of the finest theatres football has to offer. Add to that their established track record as winners of major trophies and their ability to recruit the world's top players, and you have a potent mix. Not surprisingly they were seen across Europe as the favourites to qualify for the second stage from Group H, labelled by some journalist somewhere the 'group of death' – a totally insensitive description in the circumstances. For if the challenge of taking on Milan and the proud Catalans was not tough enough, we had the extra difficulty of facing two matches against Turkish opposition just five months after two Leeds fans had been stabbed to death on our last trip to Istanbul.

In fact, immediately after the Champions League pairings were announced, rather than savouring the trips to Milan and Barcelona we had to prioritise the management and security of the games against Besiktas. It was of paramount importance that Leeds fans did not head to Istanbul in a spirit of revenge, and we were equally concerned about policing Elland Road if there was a massive influx of Turkish fans for the home game, which was scheduled first. The death of a family member or close friend is heartbreaking for all concerned in any circumstances, but to lose loved ones when they have simply gone off to watch a football match must be shattering. It is so unnecessary; a tragic waste of life.

The ill feeling towards Turkey and the Turkish around the city of Leeds was almost tangible after the dreadful events surrounding our trip to play Galatasaray in the semi-finals of the UEFA Cup in the spring of 2000. The murders of Kevin Speight and Christopher Loftus in a bar in Taksim Square in a tourist area in the heart of the city made the football match staged the next evening totally irrelevant. For the record, we lost 2–0 when we could have done better, but nobody's mind was on football that night. It simply paled into insignificance against the loss suffered by the Speight and Loftus families. Given my own experience down the years of football Turkish-style, I have always questioned how UEFA and FIFA can allow matches to be held there without demanding greater security around visiting fans, players and officials.

It cannot be deemed acceptable to ask an opposing team to run on to the pitch under the cover of riot policemen's shields to protect them from the hail of missiles and bottles cascading down from the terraces. If that kind of behaviour was seen in England, you can be assured the FA would close down the stadium. In England we would not allow thousands of supporters to effectively bring a major airport to a standstill so that a visiting football team can be bombarded with abuse by people waving banners reading 'Welcome to hell' and drawing their fingers across their throats in a threatening manner. Wonderful.

After the tragedy Galatasaray fans were banned from

attending the second leg of the UEFA Cup semi-final at Elland Road for their own safety (the Turks managed to reach the final in Copenhagen, where they defeated Arsenal to win the cup that season). Now we were faced once again with the problem of dealing with a home game against a Turkish club and with a trip to Istanbul. I was assured by the Leeds officials who discussed the high-risk security situation with the Turks that thankfully Besiktas seemed a very different club from Galatasaray. Their approach was to try to build bridges and nullify any potential hatred, whereas Galatasaray's attitude had been to whip up ill feeling to produce a powder-keg atmosphere that suited them and intimidated visitors. Sirdar Bidgili, Besiktas's American-educated president, came to England at his own request with his key directors to meet the Leeds hierarchy, and the clubs agreed that only 250 visiting fans would be allowed tickets for each game to prevent any major outbreaks of hooliganism at either match.

Nobody could have overestimated the size of the hurdles we had to overcome on and off the field, and the broader perspective of how English clubs had fared in the past emphasised the enormity of the challenge. Take Arsenal as an example. Having spent twenty happy years at Highbury, I could be accused of bias, but I do see the Gunners as a great club. Yet despite their proven pedigree, Arsenal had failed to get beyond the first phase of the Champions League, even as Double-winners in English football. Manager Arsène Wenger had personal knowledge of the continental football scene, and had recruited an array of experienced players blessed with wide-ranging knowledge of European styles and tactics, to no avail. Why should it be any easier for Leeds, especially given our draw in Group H? I remembered a Manchester United team that had done the domestic Double going down to Barcelona in a four-goal pasting.

So I didn't think we would finish in the top two to qualify for the next stage, especially given our long-term injuries and the outcome of our opening game in the Nou Camp against Barcelona. When I studied videotapes of the Catalans in action and assessed their players, I knew before we even left for Spain that we might easily be on the end of a six-goal beating – though of course I kept this to myself because I didn't want to transmit my worries to the players. It was an awesome challenge, and you need more than spirit, however unquenchable, when you're taking on world-class teams. What we needed most of all to give the Barcelona boys a real run for their money was to have our very best players available, and they just weren't. It was desperately frustrating for me.

The last straw was an incident on the Sunday before the match during a workout at our Thorp Arch training ground. Jason Wilcox, on the brink of returning to action, looked in great form as he joined in some shooting practice. There was nobody near him, but the next thing we knew, he had fallen over and broken a bone in his ankle. It was a freak injury that just about summed up our misfortunes that season.

On the way over to Spain I heard people predicting that we might get a draw at the Nou Camp. Either they were anticipating a football miracle or they were kidding themselves, because as I had feared, the game was a total mismatch. We didn't stand a chance with so many players missing. It was like going to war with a popgun. There we were, in the magnificent Nou Camp, with 97,000 spectators watching one of the richest clubs in the world taking on Leeds, average home gate around 39,000. By half-time we were two goals down and it could have been worse than that. You have to admire quality opponents and that night Rivaldo, the wonderfully gifted Brazilian, was a special talent and Patrick Kluivert, the powerful Dutch striker, demonstrated his eye for goal. At least our players refused to give up and accept a total humiliation, but the final score was 4–0, and we had been well and truly stuffed. Thank goodness the

Champions League operated on the results of individual matches rather than on aggregate scores, or we would have fallen at the first hurdle. As it was, Barcelona could not take any more from this emphatic triumph than their three points for a win, and Leeds lived to fight another day.

I love the city of Barcelona, and given the calibre of their football club, perhaps we shouldn't have been surprised to find that there is a touch of 'we'll do things our way' around the place. UEFA had brought in new rules to ensure that every ground had a pitch of the same size for the Champions League. The field in the Nou Camp is one of the biggest in Europe, and when we arrived for training we had measured it and discovered that they had not attempted to alter their standard huge Spanish league size for European action.

We quietly called over the UEFA delegate in charge of the match and pointed out the anomaly. He assured us it would be sorted out by kick-off time, but it still meant that twenty-four hours before the game we were preparing on a pitch that wasn't the right size. The next day it was supposed to be shortened by a few yards, with four yards taken off the width, but needless to say, hardly anything happened. The fact that the goalposts were in the same positions indicated that there had been no reduction in length, while in front of the main stand and dugouts only about half a yard had been taken off the width. It was a token gesture.

You sensed that Barcelona's fundamental approach was that they were FC Barcelona, and that if UEFA wanted them to compete in the Champions League they would have to accept the Barcelona way. They just did what they wanted to do. Another example of this attitude was their apparent lack of interest in adhering to UEFA's procedures for dealing with the media. UEFA appoint a stadium officer and press officer for each club. At Elland Road we developed a great rapport with two lovely Scandinavians called Lars Richt and Kjell Borgersen, smashing people who did their jobs professionally and, I'm happy to say, became great friends of our club. They made it very clear to us what our responsibilities were with regard to the media – providing players for interviews, allowing photographers into training sessions and so on, and we followed the UEFA requirements to the letter. One of these was to ensure that our players went into an area called the mixed zone for post-match interviews.

In the Nou Camp, after Barcelona thrashed us, none of their players walked through the mixed zone. They couldn't be bothered. My colleagues at Leeds made some inquiries about this, asking why we were expected to observe and respect these rules if they were going to be so openly flouted by our rivals. The response from the highest levels in UEFA confirmed our suspicion that while British and northern European clubs invariably honour the regulations, the big clubs in southern Europe do what they want regardless of the consequences. And in most cases there are no consequences, or at least nothing more than such a small fine that it has no effect on them.

So out on the field at the Nou Camp, our opening Champions League endeavours were described as those of 'men against boys'. It was a chastening experience, but it was important that I kept a perspective on the night's events and didn't become too depressed by defeat at the hands of the mighty Catalans. The key issue after a setback like that is to ensure that the players don't allow their heads to drop and are prepared properly for the next game, which was the small matter of AC Milan at Elland Road.

If I'm being brutally analytical, I think we learned several vital lessons in Barcelona. I'd say that the occasion got the better of the players. They couldn't believe how quick the opposition were, how skilfully they retained possession once they had the ball. Back at home the players' energy levels were low. During the game Lucas Radebe sustained a serious head injury that kept him out of action for several weeks. There had been real concern for his wellbeing when he was carried off on a stretcher with his neck in a brace following an aerial collision with Michael Duberry. It looked a shocking injury. Lucas was taken to hospital for X-rays and scans, and although it was bad enough, the damage wasn't quite as dreadful as we'd initially feared.

We received a great boost in the countdown to the AC Milan game with the return to fitness of midfielder Eirik Bakke and clearance for Dominic Matteo to play after his arrival from Liverpool with that knee injury. With Kewell, Wilcox and McPhail out, I needed Dominic to play on the left side of midfield to offer some sort of balance there. Eirik hadn't gained match sharpness but I knew I had to have him out on the park. The medical department warned me that either of them could break down in match action, but I had no choice. I had to play them.

To make matters worse, conditions on the night weren't the easiest for a player lacking real match fitness and full physical preparation. It seemed I might have been better advised to build an ark than a football team as the rain teemed down on that September night in west Yorkshire. The floodlights illuminated the spray that erupted with every stride as players scampered across the sodden turf. Given the appalling weather, the level of skill and technical ability on display was a tribute to both teams. And, of course, the wet conditions were particularly testing for the goalkeepers. But more about that later.

Bakke's return lifted Olly Dacourt in midfield, and I sensed that our spirit was good and that we fancied giving Milan a game. The Elland Road crowd set a standard for deafening support which they were to maintain throughout the European campaign. In the wake of our home defeats in the Premiership against Manchester City and Ipswich, as well as the four-goal Champions League drubbing against Barcelona, the relationship between the team and our fans seemed to have arrived at something of a crossroads, and they really got behind us for the Milan visit.

I had demanded a brave, courageous, committed display from my team to well and truly exorcise all ghosts from the Nou Camp, and the players responded magnificently. We never allowed Milan to settle. Nobody would dare suggest that we were in awe of them. We closed them down quickly, tracked every run by the midfield and forwards and always looked dangerous when we counterattacked. The winner came late, in the eighty-ninth minute, in fact, when Lee Bowyer let fly with a shot that even I would happily describe as speculative. Perhaps the Brazilian goalie Dida was not accustomed to the Yorkshire deluge: whatever the case, he made a hash of his effort to hang on to Bowyer's shot and the ball slithered through his hands and bounced into the net.

I thought we deserved to win, even if we had got lucky with the decisive strike. We were the side trying to get forward and trying to take the game. The mood of doom and gloom I detected before the match suddenly evaporated, and we were back on course.

One of the lasting images I have of that night was the sight of Paolo Maldini, one of the world's great defenders, wrestling Alan Smith to the ground and being cautioned for the offence. Alan had wanted to give Maldini a hard time. He respected the great Italian but he wasn't intimidated by him, and it was a great tussle. Alan won't shy away from any challenge. You really get to know what makes people tick in the dressing room just before kick-off, and you can see then that he really intends to show opponents with big reputations what Alan Smith is made of.

Another unforgettable moment was when Andriy Shevchenko, Milan's brilliant Ukrainian striker, chased through on Nigel Martyn's goal. Shevchenko did not become the most prolific marksman in Italy's Serie A by chance. He is a lethal predator and he recognised his chance to pounce. But just as the striker was ready to take aim the cavalry arrived in the shape of the sprinting Danny Mills. Danny made one of the best recovery tackles I have ever seen. He slid across the saturated turf and dispossessed the Milan striker with a tackle of impeccable timing and no little physical power.

The Milan victory was immensely significant for us. It dispelled the hint of panic around the cub after Barcelona as people wondered whether we could even finish third in the group to ensure that we at least dropped down into the UEFA Cup. There were those who had feared we would be rooted at the bottom of Group H and disappear from Europe altogether.

While we were beating Milan it was a night of surprises elsewhere in Europe, too. Besiktas defeated Barcelona 3–0 in Istanbul, and suddenly the group was wide open with all four clubs on three points. The plot in Group H was beginning to take an interesting shape and depending on our own results against Besiktas, we might not prove to be the whipping boys of the section, as some people had predicted.

Mark Viduka had missed our opening two Champions League games to fulfil his commitment to play for the Australian Socceroos in the Sydney Olympics. Although we had known about this since before he'd joined us, there were some people around Leeds who were not too pleased that he had gone, especially given our injury problems, and on his return his critics were ready to jump on him if he played poorly. Some reporters even suggested I might overlook him from selection for our third Champions League fixture, against giant-killing Besiktas, as a punishment for going to the Olympics. I never considered that for a moment. At this stage he hadn't scored a competitive goal for the club, but against the Turks that night he was magnificent as we ran riot to win 6–0 with a five-star display, delivered at a high tempo the Turks could not cope with.

Lee Bowyer epitomised our approach, and the fact that the

midfielder opened and closed our goalscoring account was a fitting tribute to his industry. The excellent Viduka, Dominic Matteo, Eirik Bakke and substitute Darren Huckerby were also on the scoresheet. For once Alan Smith wasn't among the goals, but he was unlucky not to score and was a constant source of problems to the visitors' defence. After going three up in the opening twenty-two minutes, I suppose we never looked back, but it was still significant to see Viduka operating as the power-ful, skilful target man we wanted, proving the focal point for our attacks.

Besiktas deserve credit for attempting to rebuild relationships between Leeds and Istanbul. Before kick-off, their team dis-tributed flowers to our fans in memory of the supporters we had lost in Turkey, and keeping the presence of visiting supporters so small allowed everyone to focus on the match.

Our prospects in Europe were looking brighter on the back of the two home victories: our points tally was now six from three games. Of course, because we had been such emphatic winners at home against Besiktas some people thought that an away win in Istanbul would be a mere formality. But I knew that apart from anything else, there would be a desperate need at Besiktas to regain some pride and to atone for a defeat that equalled records as the heaviest ever in the competition. And since in the Champions League each match is a one-off affair, they didn't need to beat us by six goals – a 1–0 win would do it.

When we landed in Istanbul there was no hate mob waiting for us. The security around the team coach for the ride to the sumptuous Kempinski Palace Hotel on the banks of the Bosphorus was efficient and resolute. No chances were being taken with us. It was very reassuring.

For this game I was forced to throw young keeper Paul Robinson in at the deep end because Nigel Martyn had torn his thigh muscle against Charlton the previous weekend. It was another of those freak injuries. Nobody had been near Nigel as he kicked the ball downfield and collapsed to the turf in agony. He was to be unavailable for almost two months. The promotion of Robbo for the Istanbul game understandably provoked immense debate. Many wondered if he would have the nerves and self-confidence to deal with the situation, but I was never worried about that. Weak characters tend to be found out in this environment, but young Robinson was outstanding and earned himself rave reviews. Ideally, I wouldn't have blooded him in a game like this, but I knew he had the talent and temperament to cope with the situation and on the night he looked rock solid. In the next game of our European campaign, he would be inspired.

Robbo was not the only fledgling in the side that night in the Inonu Stadium: in fact we fielded one of the youngest teams in the club's history. The average age was just twenty-two. The players were asked to display maturity beyond their years and they did so with a sense of real accomplishment.

Besiktas never looked like scoring, and although we did not express ourselves convincingly in attack, I was content with the 0–0 draw. We did squander the best chance of the game when Eirik Bakke failed to score from close range after Ian Harte's free kick landed at his feet just six yards out. But considering that we were without our first-choice goalie, centre backs, a number of midfielders and our top scorer in the suspended Alan Smith, it was a good result and set the stage for the visit of Barcelona to Elland Road.

If the Besiktas fans were not quite as bellicose as those of their rivals, Galatasaray, there was no doubting the hotheadedness with which they backed their team. We had 138 supporters with us on an official trip and, thankfully, they behaved themselves and did not fall victim to any Turkish aggression. On the afternoon of the match they were taken for a boat ride on the Bosphorus and displayed the imaginative banner 'LUFSea'. Our followers remained in resolute mood, and the only trouble came from some Turkish fans who started fighting among themselves near the end of the game.

The bad news was yet another freak injury, this time to striker Michael Bridges. After twenty-six minutes he had turned past an opponent and was sprinting forward when the Besiktas defender accidentally trod on the back of his boot, causing severe ankle damage. Within a couple of days it became clear that Michael required an operation to repair the damage and would be out for the rest of the campaign.

A victory over Barcelona would have qualified us for the second stage of the Champions League with a game remaining. As full-time approached, having maintained a 1–0 lead since very early on, we thought we had done enough – until the fourth official lifted the electronic board to indicate time added on. The Elland Road crowd heaved a collective sigh of disbelief when they saw that four minutes of injury time had been allocated. Nobody knew how the extra time had been calculated. Furthermore, according to UEFA's own records, Barcelona scored their equaliser after four minutes and thirty-seven seconds of added time. It was such a bitter setback that even in recalling the match now I am falling into the trap of allowing the disappointment of those last seconds to overwhelm what was a truly remarkable night's football at Elland Road. It was a marvellous performance in which we demonstrated that we had learned many of the lessons of our opening fixture of the competition in the Nou Camp.

Lee Bowyer maintained his excellent strike rate in Europe by scoring in the fifth minute direct from an angled free kick. The build-up to that breakthrough was a delight. Possession swept down the left flank from Smith to Matteo and Viduka. After the big striker was bundled over by Spanish international defender Abelardo, Bowyer curled an inswinging free kick over the wall and towards the far post. Barcelona keeper Dutruel appeared rooted to the spot as the ball dipped into the top far corner of his goal.

The crowd erupted. The scent of a possible victory over the mighty Barcelona hung in the air and the game was played amid a thunderous backdrop of noise, with every Leeds throw-in, never mind shots and headers, drawing the acclaim of our fans. In the second half, though, Barcelona were all over us and Robbo had to pull a string of superb saves out of the hat. After twenty-three minutes Rivaldo met Xavi's free kick with a stooping header which Paul, at full stretch, did well to claw away. He denied Rivaldo three times from free kicks and brilliantly tipped a close-range header from Alfonso over the bar. It was this save that suggested that Barca's luck might just be out and that we might pull off an unforgettable triumph. Robbo truly proved his exceptional talent that night. If he can do it against the likes of Rivaldo in the Champions League, he can do it anywhere.

But in the end Barcelona deserved a draw, and Rivaldo was the man who grabbed their lifeline. Philip Cocu had broken down the left and his cross was met by substitute Gérard's header. That effort bounced off the post, but the great Brazilian was on hand to sweep his shot home. Even Robbo had no chance this time. Although I would take issue with the time-keeping – I still don't know how the game meandered towards ninety-five minutes – we could have no quibbles about the goal. So now, having been within seconds of a fantastic victory that would have guaranteed our passage to the second stage of the competition, we needed a draw in the San Siro against Milan to eliminate Barcelona and achieve our aim.

I remember poor young Paul Robinson heading to the dressing room feeling as if Barcelona's last-minute goal had been a winner rather than an equaliser. He was just devastated, and you could understand that, but he had no reason to berate himself. He wasn't the only one. That night the referee went to a restaurant in Leeds owned by an Italian friend of mine. The restaurateur threw his watch on the ref's table and went nuts. He couldn't believe what had happened.

Unrated and Into Europe

We travelled to Milan on the back of a 4–3 victory over
Liverpool at Elland Road the previous Saturday. To this day I
don't know how we pulled off that one, but I thank Mark
Viduka from the bottom of my heart for his four exquisite goals.
For the Milan game we stayed at Lake Como in a beautiful
hotel called Vila d'Este. It's a place that is worth a visit even in
the winter. On the Tuesday night we trained in the San Siro and,
after a mix-up over transport from the team hotel which resulted
in our chairman being left behind, a new superstition was born:
that Peter Ridsdale never watches us train on the eve of a game.
I've played at the San Siro in the past and knew what to expect
of the pitch – a real bog – but it's always a shock, given the
splendour of the stadium, that they can't keep the playing surface in tip-top order. We found it as bad as ever, and the poor
surface played a significant part in Milan scoring against us.

This was the first time my wife had attended an away game in
Europe. Joy travelled with the team but stayed in the centre of
Milan with Linda Gray, Eddie's wife – in a typically kind gesture, the chairman booked them into a lovely hotel there. We
knew they were settling in well when we heard on the phone that
they had discovered the best shopping districts.

Meanwhile, amid the hype surrounding the Champions
League, came accusations that the game in Milan was a carve-
up. First the Spanish media claimed that a deal had been done
to ensure Milan gave us a draw that would put us through and
Barcelona out. Then came a counterclaim that Barca were offering Milan a collective bonus of £1.6 million to make certain that
they won, followed by an allegation that Barca had agreed to
buy a Milan player at an inflated price to cover the inducement
to the Italians to beat us. If you were a conspiracy theorist, you
were in your element. The assassination of JFK had nothing on
the English team, the Italian team and the Spaniards in a
Champions League tangle. There was no truth in the match-
fixing rumours. Milan coach Alberto Zaccheroni took the view

that the best team would win on the night, and that if Leeds got a draw against his side we would have to earn it, and that's just what we did.

In the first half of the match, Milan were awarded a very harsh penalty for handball against Gary Kelly. Kim Nielsen, the Danish referee famed for sending off David Beckham in the 1998 World Cup finals in France, pointed to the spot. Fortune was on our side when Shevchenko drove his spot kick against the post. We took the lead just before the interval, when Dominic Matteo headed home Lee Bowyer's right-wing corner at the near post. It was a crucial breakthrough for us. But after sixty-seven minutes, the cabbage-patch pitch saw Gary Kelly miss the ball as he attempted to make a tackle on the breathtakingly fast Serginho, and Milan equalised.

Paul Robinson was called upon to make a couple more outstanding saves and the closing stages were tense as we attempted to hang on to the draw. When we managed to hold out for the result that took us into the second stages of the Champions League it was a fantastic feeling. Considering that our quest had started with that pasting in Barcelona, it was a real achievement. I spotted Joy in the stadium with Linda Gray. Afterwards she told me she never wanted to attend another game like that in her life, she had been so wracked by nerves.

The result in Milan prompted one of the most unforgettable celebrations ever seen inside a football stadium. Our fans were simply delirious. When the players had showered and changed they went back out on to the pitch to salute our travelling army. The party atmosphere was heightened as each player took it in turn to sing a song taken up by the 7,000 fans crammed behind the goal. Alan Green, the BBC Radio 5 Live broadcaster, described it as 'the most powerful bonding between fans and players' he had ever witnessed.

We had a lovely party back at Lake Como that night, and the players had a singsong. It wasn't a boozy night, but everyone was just so awake and alert. I don't believe in heavy drinking sessions, but nobody was going to sleep given the excitement level in our camp, and I felt the lads deserved a couple of bottles of beer. We still got them to bed at a sensible time.

From Barcelona the flow of accusations of match-fixing continued. It was claimed that the Spanish club was incensed at Milan for letting us get through at their expense, and were calling for a UEFA inquiry. Let me assure you that there were no gifts in Milan apart from those being bought by Mrs O'Leary and Mrs Gray.

5

Life and Death

Life has a way of bringing you down to earth with a bump, and it happened to me at Lake Como. The trip to Milan meant I missed the funeral of former Arsenal star and coach George Armstrong, a great friend and a marvellous man, and for all the glory in Milan, I couldn't get over my sadness at Geordie's passing.

But if the loss of Geordie cast a shadow over events in Milan, a fortnight later I was to be faced with an experience that really brought home to me how essential it is to retain a sense of proportion.

The late Bill Shankly is often quoted as having said: 'Football is not a matter of life and death. It's more important than that.' Some of my friends who knew the great man insist that he was not speaking literally. While nobody was more passionate about their football than the manager who helped to make Liverpool the most successful club in English football history, it seems that Shanks could and would send up anyone pretentious enough to overstate the importance of the game.

I remembered this on the afternoon of 22 November when, while Leeds United were preparing for the visit of European champions Real Madrid, I was enduring a personal nightmare in our team hotel. My dad had been taken ill in Dublin. Hugh McCann, the surgeon who was looking after him, called me to say that he wanted to operate within forty-eight hours. He explained that the surgery was a matter of urgency but that as yet my father was unaware of the situation. That night we played Real Madrid in the second stage of the Champions League, losing 2–0, and the following afternoon after training I flew to Ireland to be with my mum at my father's bedside at the Mater Hospital.

I got there just as Hugh was breaking the news about the operation. He told my dad that he had been scrutinising all the test results and that it was serious. There were three bypasses to be done, plus some more complicated heart-valve surgery, that would be performed by a heart surgeon called Freddie Woods. I saw my dad push his head back into his pillow. He was clearly stunned by the news. He asked: 'Will I go home now and you'll call me back in a month or six weeks?'

'No,' Hugh replied. 'We're going to operate in the morning.'

Friday, the day of the operation, was torture. Mr Woods came to meet my mum and told her that the surgery would be long and difficult but that it was crucial to my father's chances of survival. Indeed, if they didn't perform it my dad would be dead within three months. It dawned on my mum just how serious things were, but Mr Woods was reassuring about the chances of success and she began to get to grips with the situation.

They took my dad down to the operating theatre around noon. I walked with him as he was wheeled through the hospital. It was a long, slow walk. I really, really felt for him, because he'd never had an operation in his life. He was certainly going for a major one now. It's funny what inconsequential images pop into your mind in emotional situations and stay there. One of my lasting impressions of that day was the nurse placing a plastic cap on Dad's head and me thinking: 'That suits you, Dad.' It was bizarre.

He was very sick and very worried. He had suffered two heart attacks in the previous decade and one of the side-effects of those was that he had become diabetic, so there was some concern about how he would cope with the anaesthetic and a fear that complications might set in. His second heart attack – which had happened on 15 December 1999, the day we lost to Leicester City after a penalty shoot-out in the League Cup – had been particularly serious. That was when we met Hugh McCann for the first time.

My dad had been rushed into hospital as an emergency, and when I telephoned the casualty unit my name must have made a connection with one of the doctors, because he took the call, assured me that everything would be all right and promised to look after my dad. That doctor was Hugh, and since that day he and Dad have forged a close friendship.

Now my mum, my sister Emily and I were pacing around the same hospital for hour after hour, waiting for news. In the end I volunteered to maintain the vigil, while the ladies went for a walk round Dublin to give them a break. On my own, I tried to read, but whenever the doors from the operating theatre opened I would look anxiously towards whoever emerged in case he or she had news of my dad. My mobile phone rang with people wanting information about the Leeds game against Arsenal on the Sunday, and when the nurses heard that they came and told me off for having my mobile switched on so close to medical equipment in an intensive-care area. Hugh finally appeared at 7.40 pm. He looked like he'd had a long, hard day. He and Freddie Woods told us that the operation had gone really well, and that they were delighted.

Life and Death

Eventually we were allowed to see my dad. The lovely sister in charge said by way of warning that she hoped we weren't going to faint – apparently the sight of the operating theatre proved too much for some visitors. I went in first, and I have to admit my dad didn't look too great. He was still anaesthetised in (in fact, given the heavy sedation needed for such a lengthy operation, it was two days before he really came round). My mum was shocked to see the state he was in, but at the same time she was relieved to know he had got through it and reassured by the confidence of the medical people.

That evening Hugh, one of the doctors who had literally had my dad's life in his hands, came over to me in the hospital corridor and asked: 'Do you fancy a pint of Guinness? It's been a long day.' So I joined him for a couple of pints at a pub just outside the hospital. I couldn't remember the last time I'd had a pint in Dublin on a Friday night during the football season – if indeed I ever had. It all seemed surreal. The O'Leary family's debt to Hugh is immense. He has shown real compassion and care for my dad. It was he who brought Freddie Woods on board, and we could not have asked for a better medical team. He is also very good company over a pint or two, and the black stuff tasted sweeter than ever on that emotional evening.

I spent the Saturday sitting with my dad while he drifted between sleep and consciousness. Hugh popped in a couple of times to see how he was. At around three o'clock in the afternoon a nurse switched on a radio and I listened to the latest football updates from England, reporting to my dad bits of news on how old friends and rivals were doing. It might seem daft, but I wanted to see if he would react in any way, though I couldn't tell if he was registering anything. He's told me since that he can't remember anything of that day. But if nothing else it was probably comforting for me to talk to my father about something as matter-of-fact as the football results and goalscorers.

Experiencing that twenty-four-hour slice of life in the Mater

Hospital really opened my eyes to the world beyond football. We may be battling for points every weekend, but in that coronary care ward there were people battling for their lives. For me, as for a majority of people all over the globe, the most important things in life are your health and your family, and to me personally, after those, football matters most. But when you look at the situation we were part of in Dublin that weekend, you realise that football does not bear comparison with the first two priorities.

If I'd ever entertained the thought that football was a matter of life and death, I could not have sustained it at a quarter to five on that Saturday afternoon as the results came in from England. That was when I was asked to go and say hello to a patient across from my father, who was a football nut. I was happy to oblige. That fellow was waiting for a heart and kidney transplant and was very sick indeed. How could the need for three points for any club be measured against his need? Don't get me wrong: in football terms, I give everything I've got to secure those points. When I headed back to England I wanted to see Leeds win our next game, and I'm not embarrassed to demand that of my team. But when you work in football, where winning is all-important to you, it is easy to lose sight of the bigger issues in life and you must take care not to allow your perspective to become distorted.

My mum always says I'm strong, and that I'll never realise how important it was for the family for me to be in Dublin with them for that couple of days. I still can't see it like that. I just did what should be expected of anyone in the circumstances – it was nothing special. With the operation pronounced a success, I knew my dad would want me to be back with the team for our Sunday match against my old club Arsenal but I hung on for as long as I could. I stayed at his bedside through Saturday night and flew back to England on the morning of the game. On landing, I chased home to Harrogate to get showered and changed, and then headed to Elland Road for the kick-off. My mum watched the game on television in Dublin and kept giving Dad updates of the score and the action. Afterwards she phoned me and told me she thought I looked very tired and drained. I couldn't help laughing. It seemed her belief in my strength was overdone. 'It's no wonder I'm shattered, Mum. I haven't slept for two nights hanging around that hospital.'

There is a special feeling to games between Leeds and Arsenal these days. Maybe the fact that I spent so long at Highbury as a player fuels it, but I also know that the Gunners are always desperate to avenge the defeat at Leeds in the 1998–99 season that effectively cost them the title. Nobody at Leeds had wanted to do Manchester United, our biggest rivals, any favours by handing the title to them on a plate. My team go out to win every match, and we did just that against Arsenal. We couldn't help it if Arsenal's chance was lost in the process. It all goes to show there are no dodgy games in the Premiership.

Arsène Wenger is an excellent manager and he has done a great job at Highbury. This time there was another cracking, competitive game, which we deservedly won, thanks to Olivier Dacourt's deflected free kick. It was Olly's first goal for the club and it could not have come at a better time. Unfortunately, with Leeds in the ascendancy, the atmosphere on the pitch began to change. Patrick Vieira, who I rate highly as a footballer and a man, became increasingly angered by his team's shortcomings and was lucky to escape punishment after he appeared to butt Eirik Bakke as the players waited for a corner kick to be taken. Then, soon afterwards Vieira lost out in a midfield challenge to Dacourt, his great friend and colleague in the French national side. Vieira, left on the deck, was incensed. He lashed out with his boot, lunging upwards to make contact with Dacourt's throat and jaw. It looked a wicked challenge.

Vieira was fortunate not to be dismissed. But thereafter the discipline of the visiting team declined to the point where, after the match, they surrounded referee Dermot Gallagher and the officials in the tunnel and remonstrated with them about their handling of the game. There was a lot of pushing and shoving going on. During the match I had become annoyed by the antics of Arsenal's France international forward Robert Pires, who appeared to make a meal of a tackle in front of the dugout. I admit I was wrong to take the mickey out of his free-fall display by blowing him a kiss, but the gesture hardly warranted his disgraceful reaction later on. About half an hour after the game, seeing me outside the players' lounge, he started screaming abuse at me, in full view of assembled members of the media, repeatedly calling me a 'whore'. He had to be dragged away by team-mate Thierry Henry before he could smash his way through a glass door. I was completely stunned. If one of my players had behaved towards Arsène Wenger in that manner, I would have been absolutely disgusted. In all my years in the game, during which time plenty of opinions have been exchanged with opponents and a few choice comments given and received, I have never seen anything like it. I cannot understand how blowing a kiss to a player could create the mayhem it appeared to have done in Robert Pires's mind. It was ridiculous. Leeds are a good, professional football team who play the game hard but fairly.

Inevitably, the story about this post-match rumpus leaked out. I had asked the Yorkshire-based members of the media to respect the privacy of the area they'd been in, but the story broke at the London end. I was very annoyed. On the Monday after the game I returned to Dublin with Joy and our children, John and Ciara, to visit my dad. I drove my mum to the hospital, and you can imagine my feelings when a Dublin-based reporter came over to us in the car park and asked her: 'How do you feel about your son being called a whore?'

I telephoned Arsenal's vice-chairman, David Dein, to voice my concerns about what had happened. I told him that I felt

Pires was completely out of control, pointing out that if a Leeds player behaved like that towards an opposition manager, I would view it as a serious act of misconduct, and asked him to look into the matter. But it seemed to me that David, who I have known for many years, was intent on passing the buck. He said that player discipline was down to Arsène Wenger, and that he would wait to see what his manager wanted to do about it. I felt let down by that response, and more so because David never did call me back to tell me what action, if any, had been taken. In fact such was my indignation at the incident and the resulting media frenzy that I wrote a personal letter to Arsenal chairman Peter Hill-Wood. This is not a strategy I use very often, but on this occasion I believed it was justified, and as well as communicating my disappointment I wanted to emphasise my personal regret at my own part in what had happened. I told him that I was wrong to have blown a kiss towards Pires, but that even so, I didn't feel that the gesture justified the scenes in the tunnel and afterwards.

Perhaps our letters passed each other in the post. Whatever the case, I was bitterly disheartened by the letter that arrived from Mr Hill-Wood's office at Highbury. It was handwritten on a small piece of paper and basically informed me that, given my service at Highbury, he was disappointed that I was making so much fuss about the incident. As a youngster growing up at Highbury I had been told of the standards expected from everyone connected with that great club, a football club that rightly believes it is a sporting institution. Now it seemed that nobody wanted to address the Pires problem. How times had changed.

I suppose this episode should be seen as a cautionary tale of the attitudes now prevalent in football. I think Pires had been at Arsenal about six months at the time of that game; I had spent twenty years at Highbury. It all goes to show how quickly you are forgotten.

The good news from the weekend was that we won 1–0, and

that the victory lifted my dad's spirits. He was delighted, and the medical people were delighted by the progress he was making. Ciara, my teenage daughter, was upset at seeing so many tubes coming out of her grandad, but he was just happy to be awake and able to talk to his family. The only disappointment for me was that Hugh McCann and his team all seemed to be Manchester United fans. Still, I promised them tickets for our game against their favourites later in the season.

And proof that there are supportive, caring people in the cut-throat world of football came in a call from Blackburn Rovers manager Graeme Souness. He had undergone major heart surgery himself five years earlier, and when he heard about my dad's problems he rang me and asked for my father's phone number. Later Dad called to tell me that Graeme had spent half an hour chatting to him. There was no need for Graeme to do that – it's not as if I know him that well – but it was a fantastic gesture for him to spend time on a Friday night before a vital game talking to my father. I know his words of advice did my dad a power of good.

6

The First Trial

No price can be placed on justice. But the journalists and lawyers who decided to publish the article that brought about the collapse of the trial of the Leeds players in connection with the attack on student Sarfraz Najeib at Hull Crown Court early in 2001 deserve to have some pertinent facts hammered home to them.

The trial had entered its tenth week when the judge, Mr Justice Poole, decided that the *Sunday Mirror*'s interview with Muhammad Najeib, the victim's father, as well as direct quotes from the victim himself, were prejudicial, and abandoned a case in which sixty witnesses had given evidence and answered questions from fourteen barristers. Some people described this outcome as an accident waiting to happen. The trial was so compelling, the media focus so sharp that there was always a risk that someone would forget the basic rules of contempt. In the end, the jury, by then reduced to seven men and four women, took just ten minutes to respond positively to the judge's question as to whether any of them were aware of the *Sunday Mirror* piece.

Quite apart from the cost of the court proceedings, we should not overlook the fact that the jury had been deliberating for twenty-one hours, over three days, and had already decided to acquit four of the accused on the charge of conspiracy to pervert the course of justice. We should not overlook the fact, either, that recalling the events of the early hours of Wednesday 12 January 2000 had been a harrowing experience for Sarfraz Najeib. But now a newspaper had published an interview with the Najeib family and had effectively wrecked a major trial in their singleminded pursuit of this exclusive.

The ramifications of court costs, legal fees and financial responsibilities are beyond me. Suffice it to say, thanks to those *Sunday Mirror* executives, a trial costing around £8 million had been destroyed just when the principle of justice was about to be upheld. It is a state of affairs I find truly astounding.

Let me make my position clear on the key issues thrown up by the original trial. To recap: Lee Bowyer, Jonathan Woodgate and Tony Hackworth were charged with causing grievous bodily harm to Sarfraz Najeib. Also charged with this offence were two of Woody's friends from his native Middlesbrough, Neale Caveney and Paul Clifford. Michael Duberry faced a charge of conspiracy to pervert the course of justice in connection with his role in the aftermath of the alleged attack. I told the players before the trial began on 29 January that if they had chased and brutally kicked a person, whatever the circumstances, they deserved to go to prison as a punishment.

I must also make it clear that it was four individuals employed by Leeds United who went on trial at Hull Crown Court, not Leeds United Football Club – in spite of the journalistic short-hand used to describe those four of the six defendants. The club had done nothing wrong, yet night after night I would turn on the television news and hear one newsreader after another intone: 'The Leeds United trial today heard that . . .' It was an unfortunate label and, I felt, an unnecessary smear on the vast majority of employees at Leeds who had never misbehaved in any way, let alone faced criminal charges.

Yet suggestions of a Leeds United involvement erupted in the legal arguments before the jury was even sworn in. Contained in the outline case for the prosecution was the allegation that the club had deliberately released the identities of the accused players to the *Yorkshire Evening Post* so that the paper could print front-page pictures of Bowyer and Woodgate, thereby making it impossible for them to receive a fair trial. Peter Ridsdale was named as the man who had leaked the information. It was a terrible slur on Peter's personal integrity, and a totally unfounded accusation, as was proved in the most comprehensive manner when the legal team representing Lee Bowyer called the editor of the Leeds newspaper. He agreed to give evidence and, while he refused to reveal his precise source, he did offer an explanation that forced the prosecution to withdraw their damaging claim against our chairman and the club.

On the day when the arrests were made and the story broke, Peter Ridsdale was in the Far East on business and did not receive the news until around five o'clock in the afternoon British time, at which point he ordered a statement to be released from Elland Road setting out the club's stance on the arrests. By establishing the edition times of the paper, Bowyer's lawyers were able to prove that the *Evening Post* had had a story of massive significance by around eleven o'clock that morning. There were only three possible sources for a front-page splash of such impact: the players themselves, the club or the police. I am not suggesting that the investigating officers leaked the story, but all it would have taken, as in the television programme *House of Cards*, was for somebody within the West Yorkshire force press office to be prepared to say: 'I couldn't possibly confirm those identities,' a comment which the journalist would interpret as confirming that he or she wasn't incorrect in proposing the names of the players concerned.

We knew that the players had no idea they were going to be arrested. We knew that the club didn't know either, and that Peter Ridsdale, in particular, was out of the equation for geographical reasons. From talking to Neil Hodgkinson, the editor of the *Evening Post*, we concluded that the police must have confirmed the arrests story.

There was still a difficult legal issue to be dealt with regarding the players' identities. The police had wanted them to take part in an ID parade, but the lads refused. They believed that given the media coverage and the fact that they were recognisable professional footballers, it could hardly be a useful or fair exercise. Jonathan Woodgate explained: 'As my photo appeared in every national newspaper and on television bulletins, I don't feel I can take part, as clearly any witness would have no problem in identifying me.'

The split between the legal teams representing Bowyer, Hackworth and Duberry on one hand and Woodgate on the other became increasingly evident during the trial. It appeared that somebody had come up with the plan to dissociate Woody from Bowyer and Duberry. They tried to keep Woody away from the others as the players arrived at the court, left the court and even during recesses when the lads were left hanging around in the foyer. It seemed to me, as I had sensed before the trial, that Sfx, Woody's agents, wanted to emphasise their clean-cut corporate image and were concerned with only one client in this case. The Barker Gillette team, representing the other three players, kept in touch on a daily basis, calling me every evening to brief me on events at Hull, but the first time I heard from Woody's advisers was when they were in trouble. Then one of Woody's people told me: 'If only we had worked as a team with the other lawyers.' I was staggered. It was the absolute opposite strategy to the one they seemed to have chosen.

I gathered from talking to the other lads that they rarely spoke to Woody during the proceedings. His team stayed in a different hotel from the others so that even when business was over for the day he was kept away from his team-mates in the evening, and they hardly saw him outside the dock. We hardly saw him at the training ground, either, because he opted to stay in Hull. We were repeatedly told that he needed to spend his free time on Humberside in meetings with his legal team. I have no doubt that Sfx and their legal advisers were acting entirely properly and believed at all times that they were acting in Woody's best interests, but given how close all the lads were, I thought this was a mistake. Seeing them on a daily basis, I know the way Dubes, Woody and Bow joke and laugh together, spark off each other, and they remained big mates throughout the trial. So Woody must have felt quite isolated. On the few occasions he did show up at our training ground, I realised we couldn't even consider him for match action. He looked like a ghost. The weight and muscle had dropped off him. He was completely shot through.

When the prosecution evidence was presented, I was disgusted. As counsel for the prosecution, Nicholas Campbell QC was hardly likely to spare anyone's sensitivities, but the details of the attack were appalling whichever way you looked at them. There is no way any human being should be treated like that. The victim had been chased by a pack of lads and assaulted as he lay defenceless on the ground. It was alleged that Woody had been seen to take a step back and leap with both feet in the air to land on the teenager's body. Even if our players were innocent, as they consistently maintained they were, it was awful to see them tainted by any association whatsoever with this horrible crime. As I said earlier, even if they hadn't been involved in the attack, as professional footballers with standards of behaviour to uphold, they shouldn't have been out on the town in the area in the first place.

Another revolting aspect was the allegation that Sarfraz Najeib had been bitten. He had had twelve bite marks on his face inflicted by an assailant who, it was claimed, had shaken his head from side to side 'like a dog would'. Two witnesses said they had seen Lee Bowyer bending over the victim and took him to be the biter, but forensic tests proved that it was not Bow but another of the accused, Paul Clifford. Expert dental witness Dr Geoffrey Craig explained that 'the irregular arrangements' of Clifford's teeth left him 'in no doubt' as to who had perpetrated this savage act.

The type of evidence being presented to the court sparked a new welter of hate mail and abusive phone calls to the club. The ladies who answer the telephones at any football club have to be a resilient bunch, because they are more likely than most to be faced with foul-mouthed callers determined to express their opinions. But some of the tirades over the court case, particularly during the trial, left them in tears. Even the fact that the calls were being recorded on voicemail systems didn't deter some people from pouring out vicious bile about what they wanted to do to one or more people involved at Hull or connected with the club. You could feel the hatred in their voices.

Sometimes the legitimate calls I was receiving day and night to report on progress in court didn't make pleasant hearing, either. Virtually everything that I was told by the legal eagles wouldn't happen came to pass, and everything that was supposed to be a stone-cold certainty just evaporated. Before the full trial commenced there were several days of legal argument – arguments so compelling, the defence teams confidently predicted, that the judge would decide that a fair trial was impossible and throw out the case. But as we were all to painfully discover, the trial proceeded as planned. I kept being told that one or other of the accused was about to be dismissed but the machinery just kept grinding along. It was all very frustrating.

When Woody was called to give evidence he was watched from the public gallery by his alleged victim. Woody, sitting slumped in the witness box, was reprimanded by the judge several times for mumbling his replies. I'm certain it was a traumatic experience for him, but he seemed unprepared for it. I have been told by independent observers who saw him in the dock that his performance was shocking. One evening after a day in the witness box Woody telephoned me, and I asked him how he'd done. He said his people had assured him he'd done brilliantly. That conflict of opinion really frightened me.

Woody is a smashing lad who's easily led. He can be dragged into things because he's daft as a brush. At the trial Desmond de Silva QC, Bowyer's barrister, suggested that Woody's loyalty to his Middlesbrough pals had exceeded that shown to his Leeds United team-mates, and I'd agree with that. On the dreadful night of the attack Woody hadn't been out with Leeds team-mates, he was partying with his Middlesbrough friends. As the court was to hear, one of them, James Hewison, who was not on trial, was very drunk and got into a ruck at the Majestyk Nightclub. Woody spotted his friend holding a bottle and looking as if he was about to hit someone. The club bouncers threw Hewison out, only for the trouble to continue on the steps outside when a group of Asians mocked him for being unable to hold his drink. It was Woody who tried to calm him down; Woody who tried to push him into a taxi to diffuse the situation. But several attempts to placate his friend were to no avail. I remember Mr Justice Poole pointing out in his summing-up that the comparisons made by lawyers between Hewison and a gorilla or orang-utan were 'not particularly accurate' as those animals were quiet and sensible.

Leading psychologists had warned that it was impossible to expect the players to maintain their peak form during the trial.

One of them, Carole Seheult, a clinical psychologist, was quoted in an interview: 'I would not have thought players' performances could possibly go unaffected in such circumstances. The worst thing that could happen would be if the players were left to their own devices, though I am sure experienced and big clubs would not allow that to happen with valuable stars.'

I suppose a siege mentality did begin to develop at the club. At times we didn't know whether Lee would return in time from court to play, and that was no way to prepare for matches like our Champions League quarter-final tie against Deportivo La Coruña. There had been a shadow hanging over the club for twelve months, and it intensified in the three months before the trial and during the court proceedings. It's only in retrospect that I fully appreciate the relentless pressure everybody was under. Yet we continually seemed to manage to lift ourselves to conquer any challenge on the field.

Lee Bowyer's performances for Leeds during the trial were phenomenal. His ability to deal with the situation and deliver on the football pitch was epitomised by his performance against Anderlecht in February, when the prosecution evidence was being heard. Having chased from the court to Elland Road for the Champions League match, he scored the winning goal in a 2–1 triumph with four minutes remaining. On the eve of the game, Anderlecht players had suggested that they would attempt to exploit Bowyer's temperament and he was hit with a couple of tough challenges from Bart Goor. But Lee simply picked himself up, dusted himself down and got on with the game. Any hopes the Belgians might have had of rattling him were totally unfounded. Neither Bow nor the rest of the Leeds team could have wished for greater support from the Elland Road faithful. Deafening chants of 'Bowyer for England' rang out around the stadium, especially after he had driven home our last-gasp winner to defeat the supremely confident Belgian champions.

Bow is a freak: that is the only word to describe his capacity
for producing fantastic displays against some of the top sides in
European football with virtually no training. If you let him, Lee
would play football morning, noon and night. Keeping him in
court was like caging him all week and then releasing him on a
Saturday afternoon or Wednesday night. It gave him a couple of
hours' escape from the court and all the legal argument and
allowed him to run free. Quite simply, he is the fittest footballer
I've seen in the game. How he managed it all I shall never know.
He was unbelievable.

The logistics, however, were a nightmare. Not only was he
unable to prepare for a game, but we would have to wait for a
call from Hull to find out what chance there was of him turning
up for a midweek match and then just hope he would be back
with us in time. We did investigate flying him out to Champions
League games in Europe, but the distances involved and the
necessity of getting him back to Hull for the following morning
made this impossible. For domestic home and away games we
ferried him around by car. For Saturday away fixtures, he would
turn up at the team hotel on the Friday night, have a meal and
then ring my room to make sure I knew he had arrived. We did
need to resort to a helicopter to get him from Hull to Liverpool
to play for us against Everton, but I think he was relieved he had
to do that only once, because he wasn't too keen on that particular mode of transport.

We spent hours at the club exploring ways of getting Bow to
games. I don't think any other player could have risen to the
challenge as he did, but he seemed to relish it. Perhaps the
release from the court was the boost he needed. I'm sure he was
bored there and, at times, as they all were, bewildered by the
technical legal arguments that flew over his head.

In general footballers look after themselves, and while the
staff at Leeds were all anxious that the players should be found
not guilty, the main feeling among the team was an abhorrence

of the publicity surrounding the case. They were disgusted by it, and disgusted that they were being dragged into it. Yet on Friday nights at the team hotel, they loved to see Bow back in the fold. They laughed and joked with him, and really lifted his spirits. He was the butt of much of their banter, too. But he was delighted to be back with them, and they were delighted to have him back.

What nobody knew was that just before the trial began, we diagnosed a hairline fracture to Lee's foot. So in terms of healing the injury, a spell resting in the dock and the witness box at Hull Crown Court was not the worst thing for him. But on the other hand, while he was there he couldn't receive any treatment or fulfil the kind of rehabilitation programme he would normally have undertaken to ensure his general fitness level remained high. That made his match-day displays for us even more astonishing.

In spite of his resilience, I think the pressures of the case did get to Lee. I'm sure there can't have been many times when he was not painfully aware that if he was found guilty he would face a spell, perhaps a lengthy one, in prison. I think it was after the Lazio game in the Champions League at Elland Road, when the trial was reaching its climax, that Bow seemed to linger out on the field at the end longer than usual, waving to the crowd, as if he thought it might be his last goodbye for a while. But only he knows exactly what was running through his mind at that time.

Lee Bowyer certainly grew in personal stature during the trial. But if his mental toughness shone through, the stronger he got, the more washed out Jonathan Woodgate became. The weight dropped off him and he looked terrible. Whereas playing football seemed to provide a release for Bow, Woody went the other way. I couldn't help feeling that the rapport and camaraderie Bow enjoyed by rejoining the team when he could would have helped Woody to cope better, but it wasn't to be. Not only was he unfit to play but, quite frankly, he didn't seem to want to play.

The First Trial

In the midst of one of our injury crises, I wanted Woody to sit on the bench for our clash with Lazio on 14 March, but he failed to report for the match. The next afternoon I went to play golf with two friends at Alwoodley in Leeds. In the car park I took a call from Woody. He said that he hadn't received the message that we needed him, that he was very sorry, and that he hoped his apology would keep him out of trouble with the club.

After our round and a cup of coffee with my golfing partners, I set off for home. My phone rang again. This time it was the private investigator working on the case, who said Michael Duberry needed to talk to me. I told him I was free to talk to Michael immediately, and pulled over to take the call. Michael had already told me about his predicament: that the testimony he was being asked to deliver was jeopardising his own position. Now he said that he was going home to London for the weekend to speak to his mother before giving evidence in court the next week. He was shellshocked by the trial and his family were in bits about his involvement. He didn't reveal what it was he was going to say, he simply informed me that he had decided to tell the truth even if that might not help all of the accused. He stressed that he wasn't asking my advice: he just felt it was a gesture of respect towards me, as his boss, to let me know this, because it could affect others.

As before, I replied: 'Michael, I don't know what you're going to say but all you can do is tell the truth. You owe it to your family and to yourself.' After all, he had been insisting to me over the months that he had done nothing wrong, and that there was no way he would have been sitting in that court if the truth were known. The worst thing he could have done was to have concealed the facts and got into more trouble. The truth was of paramount importance.

The team were heading for an away game at Charlton that weekend, and I invited Dubes to join the boys for the match at the Valley or in our London hotel on the eve of the game, but he didn't show up. So that phone call in my car was the last time I spoke to him before he gave evidence, and I didn't know precisely what that evidence was going to be or who might be implicated by it.

Duberry's critical spell in the witness box lasted fifty minutes. He was the last of the defendants to give evidence. Earlier in the trial, Woody had claimed that he had tripped and hurt his ankle and never reached the spot where the attack on Sarfraz Najeib took place. But Michael told the jury: 'I asked him [Woodgate] where he had been, and he said they had just had a fight with some Asians.' Duberry added: 'He was walking and talking at the same time. I didn't ask him who was involved, that was the only thing that came out.' Michael appeared overcome with emotion after delivering his dramatic testimony.

Duberry's evidence provoked outrage in some quarters and admiration in others. I'm pleased to say that the positive outweighed the negative, but this development prompted another wave of foul, abusive phone calls and letters.

One of the most laughable insinuations made during the trial was that Michael would face a backlash inside the club from team-mates and management because of the testimony he had given. There was no chance of that happening. Michael was and remains one of the most popular players at our club. As for the effect of the trial on his game, having severed his Achilles' tendon earlier in the season, he had been on the injury list. His recovery programme was halted for nine weeks and his return to full fitness undoubtedly delayed as a result. I did not for one moment underestimate the massive personal challenge he faced in giving evidence that might have compromised a friend and colleague, but I never had any fears that he would not bounce back or that the other players would disown him. I never considered selling Michael. I never even had to get him and Woody together to overcome any ill feeling or misunderstandings. They were best friends before, and appeared to be best friends afterwards. Weeks later I looked across the courtyard at our Thorp Arch training ground and saw Woody and Dubes marching back to the dressing room together, laughing like the old mates they had always been.

It was only after Michael Duberry stood up and gave his sensational evidence that I received a call from Woody's solicitor, Nick Freeman. He asked if I had known exactly what Michael was going to say. I said I hadn't, but that I had known Michael was going to tell the truth. Nick responded by claiming that, although their case was going brilliantly, it was a pity that everybody had not worked together and pooled their information. That took my breath away. According to the other players' lawyers, they had never known what Woody and his lawyers were going to say.

Midway through the trial came the dramatic news that the case against young striker Tony Hackworth, accused of joining in the attack on Sarfraz Najeib, had been dropped. Mr Justice Poole ordered the jurors to acquit him after deciding there was not enough evidence against him. A paramedic who told police that Hackworth approached him to help the badly injured victim had later said that he was 'not a hundred per cent sure' of the identity of the man who had spoken to him. Yet again the legal rumour mill worked overtime. There were also suggestions from within the court that Hackworth would not be alone in walking free: the whisper was that the cases against Woodgate, Bowyer and Duberry were on the brink of collapse. We waited to have these rumours confirmed. They never were. The trial lumbered on without Hackworth.

It was almost another month before two Leeds United players were cleared of conspiring to pervert the course of justice. Michael Duberry and Jonathan Woodgate were both acquitted on the conspiracy charge, along with two other defendants, Paul Clifford and Neale Caveney. The jury had taken more than fourteen hours to reach unanimous not guilty verdicts. As

Dubes left the dock for the last time in the nine-week trial, he stopped to hug Woody, against whom he had testified a fortnight earlier.

The jury continued to consider their verdict on the other charges. I was driving away from the training ground the day after the *Sunday Mirror* article was published when Karen Boldy, my personal assistant, called to tell me the shock news from Hull. The judge had abandoned the trial because of the danger of prejudice posed by the newspaper piece.

In the offending interview, Muhammad Najeib had expressed his opinion that the alleged assault on his son was racially motivated – even though the prosecution and defence agreed that this was not the case. Indeed, Mr Justice Poole declared: 'Justice cannot be done in the sort of atmosphere created by a publication such as this.'

In his extensive summing-up, the judge explained: 'The young man who was attacked is an Asian, and it is not in dispute that his attackers were a group of white males. What, if anything, is the significance of that? Well, let me tell you, absolutely none. We live in a time and a society where there are particular sensitivities of racism and race. But the prosecution has stated publicly at a pretrial hearing that it does not suggest that there was any racist motive in this attack.

'It is, to put it mildly, not at all desirable that a crime, and therefore a suspect, should be labelled racist when it is the prosecution submission they are no such thing. The whole misleading theme of racism, which this court thought it had exorcised, has been revived by this article. The jury has applied itself, countless witnesses have attended to their considerable inconvenience but the result is that, for now, all the effort lies derailed.'

I was absolutely gutted. I drove home in a daze. If somebody had asked me then if I could face a repeat of the trial, I would have said I couldn't. At that moment I really didn't know if I could even carry on in my job. The unwanted fallout from the whole business was affecting my family, my home life and my professional life.

I just couldn't believe we might have to face another ten weeks of public scrutiny; of people telling us how we should conduct our affairs and yet still expect us to run a football club and win matches or face criticism on that front, too. I had a really bad evening. I'm not the greatest sleeper at the best of times, but I couldn't sleep at all that night. All that money spent on the trial, all that time, everything wasted. We had to start all over again. At Thorp Arch the next day I made the mistake of complying with a request for an interview for a television documentary about football management. I should have asked for time to compose my thoughts, because I was far too engrossed in and disturbed by the outcome of the trial to concentrate on it. But instead I gave the interview and made some injudicious remarks about leaving Leeds because of the trial. Another lesson learned the hard way.

The whole business of newspaper interviews had been an issue since before the trial got underway, and in the aftermath, many attempts were made in the press to explain what had happened within the Mirror Group that had allowed the offending interview to appear, a debate which ultimately forced the *Sunday Mirror* editor Colin Myler to resign.

The Najeib family publicly complained about the timing of the publication of the interview, and protested to the Press Complaints Commission. The judge had already stated that he would be referring the circumstances of the collapse of the trial and the *Sunday Mirror*'s involvement to the attorney general. I await his findings with interest.

The director of public prosecutions also stepped into the row. He said that juries should be given greater protection from the media in high-profile cases. David Calvert-Smith QC called for wider use of the prerogative of ordering juries to stay in hotels

overnight or to otherwise remain sequestered while they deliberate on their verdicts. He explained that tighter controls were
justified when there was an 'extreme danger' of prejudice after
the jury had retired.

The legal boys insisted that the judge would decide that a
retrial was impossible and that the players would be released. It
was claimed that it would be impossible to find a jury unaware
of the developments in the first trial. I had to agree with those
sentiments. It seemed that wherever I went in the world, from
Madrid to Dubai to Rome, television networks such as CNN
were providing daily bulletins on the fortunes of the Leeds
United players at Hull Crown Court. Yet I knew deep down that
we would end up with a second trial, no matter what the legal
eagles were maintaining. And sure enough, Mr Justice Poole
announced that there would be a retrial in October 2001.

It took me a few days to get over the shock of the end of the
trial. Of course I wanted the right result for the players, but
most of all I wanted a positive outcome, a definite decision one
way or another, so that the club could move on. The retrial
meant the whole episode would drag into a third season. The
legal process seemed to grind so slowly.

Mr Justice Poole undoubtedly took a safety-first approach to
the matter, and many lawyers tell me that he cannot be censured
for that. It was unbelievably incompetent of the *Sunday Mirror*
to print their exclusive interview with the Najeib family when
they did. Under the Contempt of Court Act, of which even the
most junior reporter is aware, the media are restrained from
publishing anything during a trial which might prejudice the
verdict of the jury. Worst of all, the newspaper chose the most
sensitive issue of all – racism – on which to provoke a public
debate, and Mr Justice Poole was totally justified in his anger at
having to halt the trial. Yet I still wonder whether he could have
allowed it to run its course. The jury had sat for seven of the ten
weeks of the proceedings. They had heard all the arguments of

the learned counsels. They had heard the summing-up of the prosecution, of the defence and of the judge himself. If you accept that they might be swayed by a two-page spread in a tabloid newspaper (after all, surveys have shown that many people do not believe what they read in the tabloids), how can you assume that they will have forgotten about the furore a few months later?

In my opinion a fair retrial in front of a jury that had no pre-conceived ideas of the case seemed impossible. Such was the publicity surrounding the event that a six-month delay would make no difference. Such was the emotional content of the case that opinions were bound to be formed. And inevitably, it was after the trial had ended that the tip-off phone calls and con-spiracy theories began. The Elland Road switchboard was deluged with callers wanting to make their feelings known or, in some instances, to offer 'inside knowledge' of what had gone on. I doubt we will ever know the absolute truth.

On one hand Lee Bowyer had endured a personal nightmare in the dock at Hull Crown Court. On the other, the series of hardworking performances he produced for the club were so exceptional that he was voted the fans' Player of the Year as well as the players' Player of the Year. When the first-team squad voted for their best player, only three people were nominated. Bow won 90 per cent of the votes: a landslide victory.

At the end of each season the players are handed their shirts to keep as mementos of the campaign. They normally give them to family, friends or to a charity. Bow brought his to my office after our final game against Leicester City and left it as his gift to me. He said he had signed it, but he didn't know how he should address me on the shirt. Should it be David or Boss? 'In the end I decided I'd better not take any chances, so I wrote Boss,' he explained. 'OK?'

I've kept his shirt. It was an incredibly touching gesture.

7

Stage Two in Europe

Our European odyssey gave us the opportunity to experience at first hand the best and the worst refereeing in Europe. I have already expressed my dismay at the standards of Cypriot official Costas Kapitanis in our first European game of the campaign against Munich 1860. At the other end of the scale was Pierluigi Collina. He was without question the best.

The bald-headed Italian was in charge for our semi-final first leg against Valencia at Elland Road, and gave an impeccable display. He was authoritative, decisive and fit; he commanded respect and he gained it from all the players. I think some of them were amazed at his ability to speak clear English to our boys then aim a few well-chosen phrases in Spanish to the opposition whenever necessary.

Later in the season I went to Italy to watch the Milan derby, and who should I bump into in the hotel but Mr Collina, who later that evening produced another faultless performance. I hadn't had a real chance to compliment him on his handling of the tie at Elland Road, so I did so now. 'It's easy to caution players,' he told me. 'The secret is to referee a game without using your cards as weapons of control.' He's absolutely right.

It is widely believed in England that employing full-time referees would improve the game. I support that theory, but would add a further innovation: given the freedom of movement within the European community, I would like to see Europe's top referees offered the chance to work in England, either by signing them up permanently for the Premiership or by bringing them in on a match-by-match basis to officiate at our biggest, most pressurised games. If we can boast that the Premiership is able to recruit the world's best players, let's add to the spectacle by asking the best officials to take charge.

Many of the referees in the Champions League are better than the men we see every week in England. Perhaps this was due in no small part to the way they were encouraged to interpret the rules and control the game. Whatever the reason, they actually allowed more robust tackling and produced fewer yellow cards. If Leeds were to face a game against, say, Manchester United at Old Trafford, where the stakes were massive, I would happily fly Pierluigi Collina in for the day. I can pay him no greater compliment.

A standing joke developed at Thorp Arch whenever club secretary Ian Silvester and chairman Peter Ridsdale headed for a European draw. We used to ask Ian, who is known as the Cat, to make sure that he and Peter did their usual trick by getting us the hardest possible draw. Oh no, we'd rib them, we didn't want an easy draw, or a game that might be a formality. No, the Leeds way would be to take on the toughest and the best. They never let us down. Off went the intrepid duo for the draw for the second group stages after we knocked out Barcelona and Besiktas, back they came with a group that included Lazio, the champions of Italy, Real Madrid, the reigning champions of Europe, and Anderlecht, whose home form in European and Belgian competitions was invincible. As ever, thanks, boys.

Not even the inhospitable Yorkshire weather could knock mighty Madrid off their stride. As regular commuters from Leeds–Bradford airport we are of course familiar with the capricious nature of the climate around Yeadon. When the airfield was closed to all other airborne transport just as Real's plane was due to land we wondered where they might end up, but the kings of Europe were allowed to touch down in fog-bound Leeds and sailed through everything else they encountered just as effortlessly.

The game at Elland Road was another mismatch. My team was torn to shreds again by injuries and suspension. With Olivier Dacourt and Eirik Bakke absent, I had to use Gary Kelly on the right side of midfield and Jacob Burns in a central role. It was no way to take on the reigning champions of Europe, especially as the midfield, precisely the area where we had to make do and mend, was the department where Real were at their best. They had Steve McManaman, Claude Makelele and Luís Figo there, as well as the man I rated their star performer on that occasion, the wonderful hardworking Ivan Helguera.

In the first half we battled away and just about held our own, Jonathan Woodgate hitting the post with a close-range effort. In the second half, though, the Spaniards' class told, and they ran out 2–0 winners. Fernando Hierro, that footballing warrior I seem to have been facing for too many years, grabbed the first after sixty-six minutes. Figo took a short corner on the right, Raul played the ball back to him and when the Portuguese midfielder crossed to the far post, Hierro rose above Woody and Matteo to head home.

Two minutes later it was game, set and match to Real as Raul poached a goal from our square defence. McManaman had broken down the left and supplied Guti. His pass caught us slow and square and there was no doubting Raul's prowess as he fired low past Robinson. We gave Real cheap goals but they were absolutely clinical in their finishing. It goes without saying that if we'd had our best team out we would have given them a much better game, but after a comprehensive defeat like this it was vital to avoid descending into a mood of doom and gloom and losing our direction. There is a great ambition to beat a famous club like Real when they visit you. Such is their status in the world game that if you can take their scalp it is seen as a major coup. Conversely, we had to be careful after this setback not to become too disheartened. Overreacting to either success or failure is dangerous. I sensed a feeling that the Real defeat would scupper our European hopes and my task as manager was to keep it all in perspective, keep my head and guide the club forward.

Afterwards I bumped into Terry Venables, who was covering the game with ITV. He told me not to let myself become downhearted. A simple comparison of the players on show that night, he said, emphasised why Real should have won the game. The big issue of qualifying from this group for the quarter-finals was still on the agenda, but it was now clear that we would have to eliminate Lazio to follow Real into the last eight. And Lazio had opened their campaign in stage two by losing to Anderlecht in Brussels. We were due to meet the Romans at the Olympic Stadium in our second game in this group. Given our blank start, I knew we had to take something from it, and while Lazio were not defending their domestic title too convincingly, they were intent on making a big impact in the Champions League and in Sven-Göran Eriksson had a coach of proven international pedigree. Back home we had been slaughtered in the press three days earlier in the wake of our 3–1 defeat at Leicester City, Rio Ferdinand's debut after his £18 million transfer from West Ham. Rio was ineligible for the Lazio game, but he travelled with the Leeds squad as he attempted to settle in with his new team-mates.

I'd had harsh words with Jonathan Woodgate after his poor performance at Leicester. He had been substituted in the first half. I also spoke to the entire squad after they trained at the Olympic Stadium on the eve of the match about what was at stake. Woody's response was fantastic. He produced a brilliant display.

Inconsistency is one of the key issues you have to be aware of when dealing with young players. Their form can fluctuate from substandard to outstanding within the course of a few days. Woody didn't react to my criticism at Leicester by switching off, feeling sorry for himself and saying, 'Up yours.' He got his head right for a massive game and played excellently. Afterwards he was able to meet my eye in the dressing room and make it clear he knew he had atoned for his errors. I was happy to heap praise on him in the post-match press conference because he richly deserved it. There are too many players these days who sulk when they are criticised, however constructively. Woody wants to learn. He can be daft at times but he wants to know how to improve.

The entire backbone of our team that night was exceptional. Paul Robinson in goal produced another impeccable performance and his distribution was superb. Woody and Lucas Radebe were solid at centre back, while Olivier Dacourt bossed the midfield and in attack Mark Viduka produced a compelling performance, aided and abetted by his all-action sidekick and attacking menace Alan Smith. In fact it was one of Mark's best games of the season for Leeds. They couldn't get the ball off him.

The epitome of Viduka's creative style was the goal he set up for Smithy. When the ball was knocked into Mark's feet he seemed to hypnotise the Lazio defence as he held possession for ages on the edge of the area until, with a deft, precise back-heel flick, he squeezed a pass into Alan's path. There are those who accuse Smithy of being too hotheaded, but he was ice-cold as he side-footed the ball home for a breathtaking winning goal at the Olympic Stadium. It was great attacking play against world-class defenders. We also had an Eirik Bakke header cleared off the line by Attilio Lombardo, while at the other end, Woody undertook a similar last-ditch clearance to deny Marcelo Salas.

That 1–0 result was not only crucial for Leeds, it had a wider significance for England as well, in that it had a direct bearing on Lazio allowing Sven-Göran Eriksson to leave and accept the role as national coach. Sven is a gentleman. He is a great student of the game and always willing to share his learning with younger coaches. Nobody should underestimate the knowledge of world football Sven and his loyal assistant Tord Grip have built up over the years. They are a virtual football encyclopaedia.

That European result was a massive setback to Lazio but their manager remained a class act, typical Sven. He was totally honourable and accepted the defeat with dignity. He knew the pressure was building up on him at Lazio, but he maintained: 'It is always embarrassing losing some football matches, but I don't think it's embarrassing losing to good teams like Leeds.'

So I have immense respect for Sven, but I'm afraid I can't say the same for the coach of our next opponents in Europe, Anderlecht. Their tactical guru, Aimé Anthuenis, was rivalled only by Werner Lorant of Munich 1860 as the most self-important, aloof coach I met in Europe that season. He was utterly condescending to Leeds United, suggesting that we were little more than a pub team. We took on the Belgians in back-to-back games with the home match first. Having flown to Belgium to watch them, I realised that they would be tough opponents, and that it was important we made the most of our match at Elland Road. On the night it was a dour encounter. We didn't play well and against the run of play they took the lead in the second half, when Alin Stoica broke the deadlock with a powerful strike after sixty-five minutes.

113

We faced a massive test to bounce back, but we did just that, clinching an heroic 2–1 victory with goals from Ian Harte and Lee Bowyer. Harte's was a thunderous free kick which probably inspired the furious finale. The spirit within the side was undeniable. Instead of dipping their heads with twenty minutes remaining, they pulled together and fought like tigers. Even the equaliser wasn't enough for the boys. You could see their sights were set on one target alone: winning.

Lee Bowyer had spent the day at Hull Crown Court on trial for aggravated assault and conspiracy charges. He had rushed the fifty miles to Elland Road and with four minutes remaining was still hurtling around the pitch when he collected a pass from Alan Smith. He smashed an angled drive across the Anderlecht keeper, Milojevic, to seal a triumph that became even more important with the news from Madrid that Real had beaten Lazio 3–2 to all but end the Italian champions' dreams of European progress. Group D had developed into a straight battle between Anderlecht and Leeds for second place behind Real Madrid as the clubs prepared to move into the knock-out stages of the competition.

It was a great three points. In my opinion, six points from three games was a very healthy haul for us, but Anderlecht coach Anthuenis maintained his derisive stance. He insisted that Anderlecht would beat us easily in Brussels and that his team had deserved victory at Elland Road. The coach's attitude matched the views emanating from the boardroom, where the Belgian club's directors and officials had stunned their Leeds counterparts with their assumption that in their home match Anderlecht would walk all over us.

After the game I went for dinner in Leeds with golfer Lee Westwood, his caddie, Martin Grey, and Billy Foster, caddie to Darren Clarke. Our FA Cup elimination left us with a blank weekend before heading to Brussels, which gave us the welcome chance to prepare with precision for the second encounter with Anderlecht. It was quality time that we used properly. Knowing that I had a rare free Saturday afternoon, Lee called to invite me to join him at Lindrick Golf Club, his home course, for a knock. I took my teenage son John with me to Lee's house for a cup of tea before we all set off for the course, where we spent a lovely afternoon. Lee gave John and me better ball scores as a pair, and we beat him. It was all down to John, and to Lee's kindness.

Rested and ready to face the Belgians, we arrived in Brussels amid a welter of unbelievable propaganda being pumped out by Anderlecht. The local press claimed we would be swept aside and confidently predicted another night of beery Belgian celebrations in the Grand Place. Sometimes you have to be a little wary of how the English press translate foreign football matters. We used Olly Dacourt to translate interviews from newspapers, radio and television, where the message was entirely predictable. In a nutshell it was that Leeds United were no good and that Anderlecht's invincible home form would ensure they ran out easy victors.

The logic behind the bravado was this. Anderlecht had won twenty-one consecutive home games that season, and their last nine home European ties had also ended in victory. They were quite sure that if they could beat the likes of Lazio and Manchester United, then Leeds would pose no problems. They dismissed us completely and crudely. I'd never come up against such an attitude before, or seen a team so full of themselves on and off the pitch. It was a big mistake. I used their contempt for us as a club as part of my pre-match team talk. It's all right being offended by your opponents' words, but you still have to do the business, and we did. We ripped them apart.

We were 3–0 up by half-time and the Belgians didn't know what had hit them. They were totally shell-shocked. We played marvellously, with great movement and attacking invention. Dominic Matteo was outstanding on the left side of midfield, but this wasn't a night to single out individuals: it was a thrilling team performance. Smithy had not scored since poaching that wonderful winner against Lazio in the Italian capital two months earlier, but now the young striker put the ball away twice in the first half and worked tirelessly alongside Mark Viduka, who scored between his strikes, to establish our superiority.

Smithy's second goal, which came after some neat interplay involving Dacourt and Batty, was justifiably voted our goal of the season. His flamboyant finish as he audaciously scooped the ball over the advancing Anderlecht keeper was inspired. His first goal wasn't bad, either. The game was only thirteen minutes old when Smithy pushed a pass towards Viduka on the left. The Aussie twisted past his maker on the byline and delayed his cross for Smith to arrive in the box and dispatch a clinical volley from close range. Viduka's header emphasised his agility and ability to hang in the air. Matteo was sent scampering down the left after a good combination involving Viduka and Dacourt. The Scotland international swept over a high cross beyond the far post, where Viduka outjumped his marker before sending a looping header into the far corner of the net.

We eventually won 4–1, Ian Harte adding a second-half penalty, and afterwards discovered that, with two games in the second group stages still to be played, we had qualified for the last eight. It was a wonderful reward for a great night's work. As for Anderlecht's arrogance, it's crazy for any club to set themselves up for a fall like that. The next day one of my staff at Elland Road took a call from a top Dutch club who were hoping to play us in a friendly match. The Dutch director showered praise on us for our performance the night before and declared that after our demolition of the Belgians we would be regarded with special respect across the continent. He went on to admit that many clubs would be particularly delighted by Anderlecht's demise, because they were generally perceived as the most big-headed bunch in Europe.

The King of Peckham joins Leeds and seems happy at the prospect of moving to flat-cap country.

Andrew Varley Picture Agency

They said we were crazy to pay £18 million for Rio. Now he's acknowledged as the best centre back in England.

Empics Sports Photo Agency

Michael Duberry's season was wrecked by a torn Achilles' tendon, and his recovery blighted by the first trial at Hull Crown Court. But Dubes remains one of our most popular players and the case did not affect his friendship with his team-mates.

Andrew Varley Picture Agency

Nigel Martyn was challenged by Paul Robinson for the goalkeeper's jersey and responded magnificently.

Colorsport

My respect for George
Graham is immense, as was
my satisfaction when we
beat his Spurs side.

Andrew Varley Picture Agency

My admiration for Brian Kidd is unstinting. He is one of the top
coaches in the world.

Empics Sports Photo Agency

Our travelling support in Europe was magnificent and the players formed a special bond with our fans.

Empics Sports Photo Agency

We've made it! Our 1–1 draw in the San Siro put us through to the second stage of the Champions League and eliminated Barcelona.

Andrew Varley Picture Agency

Anderlecht had been invincible in Brussels until we arrived – and didn't we know it.

Empics Sports Photo Agency

Luís Figo of Real Madrid was eventually booked after spending the evening falling over and infuriating our players.

Empics Sports Photo Agency

Alan Smith's goal against Lazio in the Olympic Stadium sent shockwaves around the football world.

Empics Sports Photo Agency

Champions League semi-final, first leg: Gaizka Mendieta was the class act in the Valencia midfield.

Empics Sports Photo Agency

Champions League semi-final, second leg: Rio Ferdinand tackles Juan Sanchez with typical aplomb. It was Sanchez who handled the goal that set Valencia on their path to the final.

Empics Sports Photo Agency

Keane and Viduka celebrate the 2–0 victory over Chelsea that clinched our passage into the UEFA Cup for 2001–02.

Allsport

Stage Two in Europe

I don't think Leeds United had enjoyed a greater standing in European football for many years. While other more vaunted clubs were still battling to make it to the quarter-finals, we had the luxury of travelling to take on Real Madrid in Spain and entertaining Lazio at Elland Road in the knowledge that we were merely fulfilling fixtures. I don't mean to suggest that we didn't care about the outcome of those games – nobody who saw them could have doubted how committed we were to winning.

Sadly, at the Bernabeu we were denied a famous victory over Real Madrid by a deliberate handball from Raul that went unpunished by the Polish referee Ryszard Wojcik.

At least Wojcik was decent enough to visit our dressing room and apologise personally to each angry member of our team for his gaffe in the wake of our 3–2 defeat, having watched television replays of the incident. It was a magnanimous gesture, and I salute the referee's honesty in owning up to his mistake, but what I still found galling was what was highlighted by the television replays: namely that he was perfectly placed to spot Raul punching home Luís Figo's free kick with a 'goal' reminiscent of Diego Maradona's 'Hand of God' strike against England in the 1986 World Cup.

We had taken the lead after just six minutes when Lucas Radebe supplied Viduka on the right flank and the increasingly impressive partnership of Viduka and Smith delivered the goods again. Big Mark crossed into the middle for Smith to run on to his pass and steer a shot beyond César in the Real goal. We were in total control of the game when Raul struck two minutes later and you could see the sense of injustice on the face of Nigel Martyn as he chased the referee to protest. If Nigel felt cheated by that effort, he was dumbstruck by the next – a cross from Luís Figo that exploded off a divot like a Shane Warne googly and left the goalie stranded.

We were back on level terms early in the second half when

Harry Kewell won a corner with his persistence on the left. Harte took the kick and, catching the Real defence dozing, Viduka headed home from close range. Perhaps the fact that both teams knew they had qualified for the last eight encouraged an open, attacking game but I felt we could pull it off until Figo and Raul combined again, this time to create and score a legitimate goal. Even so, we refused to be downhearted. In the closing stages Smith set up Viduka, whose angled shot hit César's left-hand post.

So Real had achieved the victory they wanted, and in the closing stages Makelele and Figo both conveniently acquired bookings that would bring them one-match bans and thus rule them out of the academic tie against Anderlecht. They would be free again for the knock-out stages. Figo seemed to have been trying hard all night to arouse the referee's anger. We couldn't take a free kick without the Portuguese star trying to encroach and block it. In the end even the tolerant Mr Wojcik could no longer stand the player's verbal dissent. He could have brandished a yellow card much earlier for persistent diving.

In the aftermath of the game UEFA handed Raul a one-match ban and fined him £8,000 for his unsporting behaviour. A UEFA appeals committee eventually overturned that punishment, ruling that they could only act if the referee had been unable to make a factual decision. Referee Wojcik said he had decided that Raul had used his head to score. Apparently, that made it a factual decision.

So we lost to Real again, but this time we had given them a real game. You couldn't doubt the determination of our team, and there was a genuine sense of injustice about how we'd been beaten. Now we were left with a supposedly meaningless game against Lazio to fulfil our Champions League group stage commitments. When each club is paid a £300,000 bonus for winning you can't ignore the need to pursue a victory, but it was of course sweet for us to be able to prepare for such a prestigious game without being under any pressure to produce a positive result. As I looked at the bigger picture of the success we were aiming for at home and abroad, I decided to rest certain key players for the Lazio visit. Paul Robinson was recalled in goal to give Nigel Martyn a breather while in midfield David Batty and Olivier Dacourt took a break and I gave games to Jason Wilcox, Jacob Burns and Alan Maybury. I know there was some disquiet in the club that we might take a thrashing against the Italians, but I was confident there would be no major embarrassment.

One of the traditions of European games is that the directors of both clubs, together with the UEFA officials appointed for the game, meet up at either an eve-of-match dinner or a pre-match luncheon. The managers or coaches of the teams and the referee and his assistants do not normally attend, so I was delighted when my wife Joy and I were invited to be part of the pre-match formalities for Lazio's visit. The dinner took place at Harewood House, the home of our club president, Lord Harewood, who is a knowledgeable football man, a great fan of Leeds and has gained a great insight into the football industry during his lifetime. He and Lady Harewood are renowned hosts, so it was with eager anticipation that we set off for their stately home near Wetherby to meet the Roman delegation.

You could see that the Lazio hierarchy were stunned by the beautiful surroundings as well as by the excellent food and wine served at the table. It was a wonderful evening, featuring witty speeches delivered in an atmosphere of genuine bonhomie. Our chairman, Peter Ridsdale, is a great ambassador in these situations and the Lazio directors accepted the low-key nature of the game with good grace. One of them even managed to invite me in his halting English to visit Rome for their derby game against Roma. It was an invitation I took up later in the season and I have to admit that it was, as the Lazio director promised, the most incredible derby encounter I have ever witnessed. It topped even the Glasgow rivalry between Celtic and Rangers for colour, noise and passion. That's how intensely football runs in the veins of the Romans.

Back at Elland Road, Leeds and Lazio competed with conviction and there was no hint of anybody taking it easy. Even with the changed team we wanted to win and the crowd gave the players a standing ovation after the 3–3 draw. Lazio took the lead after twenty-one minutes through Fabrizio Ravanelli. We responded positively: seven minutes later Lee Bowyer chipped an angled shot exquisitely over Luca Marchegiani for a fabulous equaliser. Unfortunately, however, we allowed the visitors to regain the initiative immediately. This time Matteo was adjudged to have fouled Ravanelli and Sinisa Mihajlovic made no mistake with his penalty. We pressed forward in pursuit of a second equaliser, which came with a spectacular flourish, thanks to Jason Wilcox's far-post volley, and after the interval Viduka put us ahead with a fine header from Harte's free kick.

In Italian football people claim Mihajlovic is worth his place for his ability in dead-ball situations alone. He takes all Lazio's free kicks, orchestrates their set pieces and lashes home their penalties. I'm dubious about whether that armoury in itself should guarantee a player his place but, as if to emphasise that what he does well he does brilliantly, it was the Yugoslav who scored Lazio's last-minute equaliser with a well-struck free kick from the edge of the area. However, on the balance of play in the second half I think we deserved to win, and certainly Mihajlovic's free kick should never have been awarded. In the attack that led up to it Pavel Nedved felled Alan Maybury with a wild, two-footed challenge. It was a horrendous tackle, meriting an automatic red card, and how the referee missed it I will never know. I will also never know, either, how Alan avoided breaking his leg. He was making his first senior start for three years, and he was lucky not to have suffered an injury serious enough to keep him out for another three.

In keeping with the mood of candour and apology we had

enjoyed in Europe, Nedved did at least take the trouble to come to our dressing room to apologise to Maybury for the challenge.

All in all, though, given the team we put out, a draw was not a poor result, and it was heartening to hear the crowd's reaction to our performance. They were obviously pleased with a six-goal thriller, even if victory had been snatched away from us at the end.

There were three English clubs in the last eight of the Champions League, and we knew we could not meet either of the others, Manchester United and Arsenal, at this stage. We also couldn't be paired with a club we had faced in Group 2 of the competition, so that ensured that we would be kept away from Real Madrid. The number of potential opponents, then, was somewhat reduced as we perused the options. It was interesting to see that the Spanish league had matched the Premiership in providing three quarter-finalists, an indication of the burgeoning status of Spanish football in the wake of the previous season's final between Valencia and Real Madrid.

We were paired against one of them, Deportivo La Coruña, the reigning Spanish champions. It was not the draw we wanted for several reasons. Deportivo had won their league with such a precocious mixture of flamboyant attacking and breathtaking goals from their imported forwards, Brazilian playmaker Djalminha and Roy Makaay, the prolific Dutch striker, that in the countdown to the game I said I could hardly believe I was talking about the potential of Leeds reaching the last four of Europe's top club competition. It was the stuff of fantasy. I was no less aware that earlier in the competition Deportivo had displayed incredible tenacity and self-belief to turn around a three-goal deficit against Paris St-Germain and grab a momentous win. Clearly, if the team from Galicia on Spain's north-west coast got some attacking impetus going, they had the ammunition to cause problems for any opponents.

For their part, Deportivo admitted that they were pleased to

121

be playing us. I have to say that I couldn't blame them. In terms of European experience and status we were undeniably the least daunting of the seven potential opponents left standing, and given that the games on the route to the final were being played over two legs on aggregate scores, this was a great chance for Deportivo to bolster hopes for another season of Spanish domination.

The fact that Deportivo saw us as the weakest team left in the competition inevitably provoked headlines linking us with the cult television programme of the time, *The Weakest Link*. It was a jibe our fans took up with relish during the first leg at Elland Road. Because our performance in the quarter-final first leg at Elland Road on 4 April was quite stunning; our best home performance as a unit of the season. We were strong and competitive and we took our goal chances well. We seized the initiative and played high-tempo football that constantly troubled the visitors. I knew we would need a good lead to take to Spain, and I couldn't have asked for more than the three we scored. But what I told my players before kick-off was that it was critical we didn't concede an away goal, and events in Spain thirteen days later bore me out. Yet there was no doubting the irresistible nature of our football in that first leg. On my way home I took a call on my carphone from Gérard Houllier, the Liverpool manager, who was out of the country preparing for a UEFA Cup tie. He had seen our game on television and was moved to call to congratulate us on a perfect display.

We were in front after twenty-six minutes when César conceded a free kick for a foul on Alan Smith just outside the penalty area. Those who consider David Beckham, Rivaldo and Roberto Carlos as the free-kick kings of Europe should have seen the emphatic way Hartey smashed in his unstoppable shot, via the underside of the crossbar, to blast us ahead. We might have doubled our lead just before the interval, but unfortunately, Smithy seemed to see Harry Kewell's cross a fraction late and miscued his header wide. He atoned for that miss early in the second half by powerfully heading his fifteenth goal of the season, and his fifth in Europe, past Molina. This time Harte had provided the cross from the left flank. Alan timed his run into the box to perfection and planted his downward header into the net.

Thankfully we didn't sit back and attempt to protect a two-goal lead. Instead we scored again after sixty-six minutes with Rio Ferdinand's first goal for the club. After Harte's corner deflected off a defender's head, Rio arrived to send a flying header into the roof of the net. That goal sealed a fantastic night's work.

Many people think that managers are too quick to play down emphatic first-leg leads when the away tie has yet to be played, but I have no doubt that the grave words of caution I voiced after the game were totally justified. Inside their compact, noisy stadium, Deportivo were quite capable of pulling off a coup, and their belief in their own football ability and destiny made them extremely dangerous opponents. If football fans around Europe seriously rate only Real Madrid and Barcelona as real super-powers in Spanish football, they should not underestimate La Coruña. In terms of attacking football and goalscoring endeavour, coach Javier Irureta had put together a magnificent side and, having watched some of their thrilling goals in Spanish league matches, and from the scouting reports we had compiled on them, we could not fail to be aware that they had the firepower to make life difficult for us. In the previous thirty-one matches played at the Riazor Stadium, only AC Milan had been winning visitors.

It was twenty-six years since Leeds United had last reached the semi-finals of the European Cup, with the post-Don Revie team guided by Jimmy Armfield to the final in Paris, which they lost in controversial circumstances to Bayern Munich. Our three-goal lead notwithstanding, I knew it would be an exacting test of our collective talents to knock out Deportivo.

Flying out on the Monday morning to La Coruña, infamous as the wettest place in Spain, we were in for a pleasant surprise: the weather was glorious. We were booked into a very hospitable hotel that had been recommended to us, overlooking the bay. We could see the stadium across the water, and I guess you could have walked there around the promenade in twenty minutes. The climate was perfect for convalescing from a few bumps and bruises and made us all feel as if we were enjoying a mini mid-season break. Before the kick-off, I prepared the lads with a walk along the sea front and then rested them.

The warm weather had nothing on the temperature on the night of Tuesday 17 April inside the Riazor Stadium, a tight little ground with a good pitch. We had been right to foresee that their spectacular fightback against Paris St Germain would have inspired in Deportivo a belief that they could pull off another football sensation. That kind of collective conviction within a squad of players is a priceless commodity. If they are truly confident that they can turn that kind of deficit around, they are off to a flying start. Indeed, on the eve of the game Irureta had said: 'Miracles can happen in football.'

Thankfully, this wasn't a venue in which we had to win, but we still had to be careful how we handled the game. And in the opening exchanges we probably played as poorly as we had in Europe since that early trip to the Nou Camp and the 4–0 battering by Barcelona. Whether it was a touch of tiredness setting in, or there was a bit of a hangover from our historic victory over Liverpool at Anfield the previous Friday I don't know, but this was the first time I sensed apprehension among my players. They seemed to be handicapped by the awareness that they were so near to the semi-finals and had that three-goal insurance policy. The job might have been nearly done, but they still had to see it through. We started the game by standing off the Deportivo players and sitting too deep in defence. We invited too much pressure. The game was only eight minutes old when

124

Italian referee Stefano Braschi decided that Harry Kewell had pushed Victor and awarded the home side a penalty. My players were not happy about it, but Djalminha had the ball and he bided his time before stroking a low spot kick past Nigel Martyn.

It was game on now. I had a pop at the boys at half-time and we tightened up our organisation. We looked better at the start of the second half but fell asleep when Deportivo won a free kick outside our area. There were still seventeen agonisingly long minutes remaining when substitute Diego Tristan side-footed a low shot home at the near post from the quickly taken free kick. That set the scene for a nerve-shredding finale to the game. I didn't keep the statistics myself, but I'm told that Deportivo had made twenty-one attempts on our goal and hit the woodwork three times in the game. We couldn't have afforded any time to be added on the way things were going, because there would have been only one winner, and it wouldn't have been Leeds.

Forced to stage a desperate rearguard action, we had a few heroes out on that field in north-west Spain, but none greater than Alan Smith, who ended up chasing back into his own penalty area in the dying minutes, where he made a sliding tackle to deny a clear-cut scoring chance. It was a tackle to which I would have been delighted to put my name in my playing prime.

That night Smithy epitomised the spirit I demand from my team. As I had warned, Deportivo had the pace, power and belief to score three goals against us. That we kept them to two was partly a matter of good luck, but it was a just reward for our emphatic first-leg victory at Elland Road. That was the performance that took us into the semi-finals. I never like losing, but people told me I had to look at the big picture this time, and we were through to the last four of Europe's top club competition. I suppose that's the perfect answer to a football riddle. When can losing be fun? When you reach the semi-finals of the

Champions League. And it was a fantastic feeling – especially as we were the only English club to reach the last four: Arsenal had bowed out earlier in the month and Manchester United exited the following night.

The day of our Champions League semi-final first leg at Elland Road, 2 May, was my forty-third birthday. It was also twenty-eight years to the day since I had come to England from Dublin in the hope that I could make a career as a footballer. If you'd asked that callow Irish youngster whether one day he'd be managing a team in the last four of Europe's top competition he would have answered honestly and firmly: 'No chance.' Karen Boldy, my PA, arranged a surprise party for me after the game. My dad, well on the road to recovery from his major heart surgery, came over with his surgeon, Hugh McCann. It was lovely to see so many old friends, though it would have been even better if we had crowned the day with a victory: the match had ended in a goalless draw.

The home tie was the first of three tough games in the space of just seven days, all of which would have a defining impact on the outcome of the season. We were meeting the previous season's Champions League losing finalists at home and away either side of a demanding trip to Arsenal, who were still in need of points to clinch their passage into the European competition in 2001–02.

I had immense respect for Valencia and for their coach Héctor Cúper, who moved on to Inter Milan in the close season, a wily Argentinian famed for his defensive organisation. None of his teams ever concede cheap goals. They make you work for your openings, so when you get one you have to be clinical or live to regret your profligacy. In centre backs Roberto Ayala and Mauricio Pellegrino Valencia had a formidable duo who took no chances and no prisoners. Ayala, in particular, was ruthlessly efficient. The publicity surrounding the tie was immense. I felt that our international profile was growing, and this was important for us if we were to market Leeds United FC globally and attract better players from around the world.

I'd had loved to have scored a few goals, but at the same time I was desperate to ensure that we didn't concede an away score. Both teams hit the woodwork, Gaizka Mendieta, Valencia's outstanding midfielder, heading against the bar in the first half, a feat emulated by Lee Bowyer in the second. I think we just about deserved to win, but we still needed a smart defensive header from Rio Ferdinand in injury time to save us from a Spanish mugging when substitute Vicente miscued a speculative shot from the left. The ball reared up and sailed over Nigel Martyn's head, but just as it looked as if Valencia were going to triumph with the cruellest of flukes, Rio chased back on to his own line and leaped under the crossbar to head the ball away. It was a great example of athleticism and anticipation.

Earlier it had seemed that we might break the deadlock with a set piece. For instance, when Lee Bowyer flicked on Ian Harte's corner early in the second half, he set up an opportunity for Dominic Matteo to plant a firm, downward header towards goal. Unfortunately, Santiago Cañizares responded well and scooped the effort away with his left hand. And six minutes before the interval, Harry Kewell met Harte's free kick with a header across goal which Rio flicked on towards the far post. Alan Smith appeared to be unmarked and ready to pounce but, sadly, from close range he headed wide.

Mendieta was a real handful on the Valencia right flank, hard-working and skilful, with a great eye for creating space for himself to deliver exquisite defence-splitting passes and invite crosses for his forwards. You could see why he was hailed as one of Europe's leading midfielders. In terms of operating on the right flank, he was up there alongside David Beckham.

The 0–0 draw was a disappointment but not a body blow. We knew we would have to go to Spain and at least earn ourselves a score draw, but after travelling to Rome and Brussels and emerging victorious, as well as pulling off that 1–1 draw in the San Siro against AC Milan, we were not without hope. The counterbalance to this optimism was that on our previous three trips to Spain we had been beaten, by Barcelona, Real Madrid and Deportivo La Coruña respectively.

After the tough Premiership game at Highbury on the Saturday, we stayed overnight near St Albans to give the players a chance to rest before travelling to Spain for the second leg. It was there that I received a call on the Monday afternoon with bombshell news from UEFA. Although Pierluigi Collina, the world's top referee, had chosen not to punish our player during the match, Lee Bowyer had been spotted on television in a clash with Valencia's Sanchez in the first leg, and UEFA's disciplinary commission had decided that he must serve an immediate three-match ban for violent conduct – a ban that would exclude him from the second Valencia game and from the final, if we were to reach that stage. I was stunned. We couldn't afford to lose Lee, and it was a terrible blow for him as well as for our chances. We studied the video. It was ludicrous to claim that Lee had stamped on his opponent: the Valencia player had fallen under-neath him, and the only genuine contact was when Bowyer accidentally trod on the Spaniard because he couldn't avoid him.

My incredulity at UEFA's action was heightened when I wit-nessed, along with millions of other viewers, an incident in the semi-final between Real Madrid and Bayern Munich in which Mehmet Scholl, the Bayern midfielder, blatantly smashed his elbow into Michel Salgado's face as he waited for a throw-in to be taken. The offence merited an automatic red card but the ref-eree missed it. What would UEFA do with this, I wondered, especially since Bayern went on to clinch a place in the final? Surely Scholl would have to be banned for the mandatory three games for violent conduct? The video evidence was absolutely conclusive, yet UEFA bottled their decision. They announced that as Salgado was standing behind Scholl it was impossible to prove that the German international had acted with malice. If smashing an elbow into an opponent's face while you wait for a throw-in can be deemed to be an accident, it makes a laughing stock of the whole disciplinary system.

And if video evidence could be used to punish Bowyer, it's a pity UEFA wouldn't call upon it to analyse controversial goal situations. We started quite well against Valencia but the warning signs were there after just three minutes when Nigel Martyn was called on to make a good save from Mendieta. They took the lead after just sixteen minutes with a goal from that man Sanchez that was clearly a handball. If he wasn't quite as blatant as Real Madrid's Raul had been a few weeks earlier, there was no doubt that the Valencia forward had used his arm to deflect a driven cross from skipper Mendieta, the blond Spaniard who was inspirational to the home side as he made his 300th appearance for the club.

We battled on, and at half-time I told the lads that realistically nothing had changed. We only needed to score one goal to get through to the final. Provided, of course, that we didn't concede any more, it was as simple as that. I believed we could do it, but we went out in the second half and just fell to pieces. We gave away a poor goal immediately after the interval and then let in a third in the fifty-second minute. It was a heartbreaking way to go out of the competition after so many moments of unbridled glory.

If we could dispute Valencia's opening goal, we gave them their second on a platter. It was Sanchez again. This time we backed off suicidally as he collected possession and raced forward. Nobody attempted to close him down as he fired a low shot from twenty-five yards past Nigel Martyn. It was a cheap goal to give away in such a precious game. Mendieta had actually let us off a few minutes earlier by overrunning Aimar's pinpoint pass, but he made amends with Valencia's third, driving home a powerful shot with his left foot.

As our dream was dying in the cacophonous Mestalla Stadium, there was a thought bugging me. I could see that Alan Smith was becoming increasingly exasperated by events and I looked at our bench in search of a substitute. We had no strikers available. I was worried that with his will to win he might do something daft out of frustration. He did. He launched into a two-footed challenge on Rodriguez Vicente that left the Swiss referee Urs Maier with no option but to send him off.

It was down to young, competitive stupidity. I had a right go at him in the dressing room at the end. I walked in and saw Alan crying. I made him cry even more when I pointed out that he would feel real hurt the next season when the European games came around again and he found himself suspended. I knew how much he loved to play, and he had proved a marvellous 'football warrior' for us all season, yet here he was withdrawing his services through indiscipline. What he did was no good for Alan Smith, for his team or for me, his manager. I left him in no doubt about that.

So for Leeds, Europe was over, and it goes without saying that we were all bitterly disappointed. In the aftermath of our defeat I had media matters to deal with, as ever, and a message was relayed to the dressing room asking our players to walk through the media mixed zone for interviews. As you can imagine, the mood in the camp was not one that immediately generated bonhomie and chit-chat with journalists. Normally in these circumstances, perhaps two or three of the more self-confident, experienced players will take it upon themselves to offer a few words and spare the others. At some clubs nobody will venture into the midst of the press. But coach Brian Kidd turned to the lads and said: 'We want to win with style, so let's show we can lose with style.' And with that, every single Leeds player marched through the media mixed zone. It was a clear statement that they could handle defeat as well as victory. I know many onlookers were both staggered and impressed by that collective post-match display.

Our quest for European triumph had lasted nine months. It started on 9 August 2000 and ended on 8 May 2001. Nobody had thought we would come close to real glory – so near and yet so far. We had travelled 17,100 miles across Europe making many friends, maybe a few enemies, but undoubtedly spreading the word that Leeds United had to be recognised as one of the burgeoning talents in the world game. It had been an unforgettable adventure. There was something symbolic, too, about the fact that on the night it all ended we couldn't find the police escort scheduled to guide us to the airport and were forced to sit on the team coach watching the ecstatic people of Valencia go wild with jubilation.

Throughout our campaign, wherever we were and whoever we were facing, the questions from journalists would be largely predictable – in particular the one about what I considered to be our most significant victory. Was it Lazio away or Anderlecht in Brussels? What about smashing six goals past Besiktas in a record-equalling triumph? My answer, I think, left my inquisitors dissatisfied, but it was the truth. It was the answer I have already given at the start of this account of our European odyssey. That the moment of European glory I savoured the most was our first: the qualifying round against Munich 1860, when our squad was devastated by injuries and I had to field perhaps the weakest team of the season. The fact that we knocked out the Germans with our resources at breaking point was hugely significant to me. That win may have lacked the spectacle of later victories, but it was a tribute to my players and to our collective will to win. And it was a win that sent us on a journey across Europe which nobody connected with Leeds United will ever forget.

8

Kiddo, Rio and My 'Feud' With Fergie

As we launched our assault on the quarter-final stage of the Champions League, I realised that I needed somebody alongside me to share the coaching duties. I was concerned that the players were hearing too much from me; that having them listen to the same voice day in, day out would reduce its effectiveness. I felt I might make a bigger impact if I devoted shorter, more intensive periods – 'quality time', if you like – to working with the lads.

So, in the countdown to our game with Manchester United on 3 March, which was a must-win occasion for us in the Premiership, I promoted Brian Kidd, our director of youth development, to head coach of the first team. There were those who interpreted the timing of his appointment as an attempt by me to wind up Sir Alex Ferguson, for whom Brian had worked at Old Trafford. That suggestion was rubbish. If people thought

Brian's promotion might affect Alex and Manchester United as they prepared for a trip to Elland Road, they were deluding themselves. By then the Mancunians were safely on course to win their seventh Premiership crown in nine years, which would reinforce their standing at the summit of the English game.

It is well documented that Brian left Old Trafford to become manager of Blackburn Rovers, and soon after that Alex published his autobiography, in which he was very critical of Brian. The vitriolic tone of Alex's comments stunned many people at Old Trafford as well as managers and coaches elsewhere. I don't know the ins and outs of what happened between Brian and Alex. Brian is a man who doesn't say too much about the past. He respects personal privacy – you can tell him anything and know it will go no further – and I respect his.

There was apparently one embarrassing moment after Manchester United's visit to Elland Road. I understand that Alex came into the coaches' room for a drink while Brian was in the shower, and that when Brian emerged, you could have cut the atmosphere with a knife. Brian quickly changed while Alex just kept talking, and never blinked an eye as Brian walked by. I just thought it was a sad way for two men to behave after all they had shared at Old Trafford, and vowed that I would never let it happen to me. I hope that in ten years' time Brian and I will have shared the sort of glory he and Alex savoured at Old Trafford, and I believe we will be true and trusted friends for that experience.

Brian joined Leeds in the summer of 2000 when we decided to revamp our youth set-up. His impressive track record as the man who established the Manchester United youth programme before being promoted to work with the first team, where he continued to nurture many of the youngsters he had signed, is second to none. But after a brief, unlucky spell as Blackburn Rovers manager, Kiddo was available for employment, and he was the kind of jewel we couldn't afford to miss. I had first got to know him as a youngster at Arsenal, when he joined the club in 1974. I liked him then and have watched his coaching career with growing admiration.

I decided to ask Brian to move from youth development and become our head coach after a telephone conversation with Gérard Houllier. I took a call from the Liverpool manager on my mobile phone as I was rushing through Brussels Airport after a scouting mission to watch our Champions League opponents Anderlecht. I told him I was chasing the plane to get back to our training ground, having put training back by an hour so that I could be with the players. Gérard warned me I couldn't do everything and that I'd kill myself if I carried on with this kind of schedule, racing from hotels to airports and airports to training grounds. He explained to me how he handled things at Anfield. He helped to plan every training session, but there were times, he told me, when he needed or wanted to step back and observe.

I was concerned about the limited opportunities I had to watch other teams, sometimes abroad, and players in action. I have a good scouting system, but I do not sign players solely on the basis of recommendations or videos. I insist on watching any potential signing in the flesh, so to speak, because the buck stops with me. And if I am to kick the club forward in the way I think is right, it's vital that we keep abreast of the latest tactical and training initiatives from around the world. To do this a manager has to see games and meet people.

I thought about my backroom staff and the ramifications of a reshuffle. Brian would be ideal as head coach, but he needed to switch roles at the right time. I didn't want to announce his appointment when we had lost a few games in case it was seen as any reflection on Eddie Gray, my assistant manager, who does a great job. Originally I decided to hang on until the end of the season. Then, after we beat Anderlecht 4–1, I thought, why wait? I don't like putting things off. Why not get Brian involved with the first team now? We couldn't have been riding higher: we were through to the last eight of the Champions League.

I talked to Brian about the move before he went away with England for an Under-21 international against Spain, working alongside Howard Wilkinson. He was stunned. Brian had been careful never to show any ambitions as regards the Leeds first team. He didn't even come to watch our games. He would attend the youth games then go home and watch us on television. He concentrated solely on overhauling our youth set-up. He asked for time to think over my offer. He did not want it to look as if he had stitched anybody up. I told him that he could look anybody in the eye without embarrassment. He had not manoeuvred any situation to suit himself – it was my decision to put him in charge of first-team coaching, and I thought it was a role to which he was ideally suited.

Brian loves coaching and I knew he would revel in working with the first team. I'd watched from a distance how senior players related to him when they bumped into him at the training ground. I also knew from personal friendships with the likes of Roy Keane and Ryan Giggs at Manchester United what they thought of Kiddo. After a training session I told Eddie that Kiddo was to be the new first-team coach. I think he was surprised, and perhaps wondered what he was going to do, but there was still a role for Eddie, and he wasn't being demoted. He remains my assistant manager, assists me in anything I want to do and helps Brian with the coaching as well. He still has an input in team affairs and his football knowledge deserves respect. He has done sterling work for me and I admire his loyalty to the Leeds cause.

It's sometimes easier to avoid making decisions rather than taking a new direction that can create ripples. I had dinner soon after Brian joined the first team with Everton manager Walter Smith. He said he respected my initiative and believed, as an outsider, that I had done the right thing for the club. I told him that I could have sat tight – nobody would have known any different with us flying high in the Champions League and climbing in the Premiership – but I knew that a change was needed for the benefit of the club, and so I had to make it. It would have been a mistake to have let things drift. All the same, Brian's appointment did create a few shockwaves.

Although the timing was coincidental, it was an interesting weekend for him to take on his new job. After all, nobody outside Old Trafford knows what makes United tick better than Kiddo.

When I had mapped out my plans in the run-in to the season, I had acknowledged that if we were to pull off a sensational climax to the campaign we had to be looking for three points against the champions elect. I feared that anything less would cost us a place in Europe's premier club competition. I was to be proved right – and in highly controversial circumstances. Our control of the game during the first half was so absolute that the visitors did not manage a single worthwhile shot on our goal. But then, just before the interval, came the incident that was to provoke hundreds of headlines. Fabien Barthez, Manchester United's World Cup-winning goalkeeper, clearly stamped on Ian Harte after an aerial challenge. There was no disputing the validity of the penalty awarded to us. The only question in our minds was how referee Graham Barber would punish the goalie. Would he produce a red card or a yellow one? FA guidelines state that violent conduct is an automatic sending-off offence. Even Sir Alex, in his post-match press conference, admitted that if Barthez had stamped on an opponent, he should have been dismissed. Unfortunately for Leeds, the referee allowed Barthez to stay on the pitch and to rub salt in our wounds by saving Harte's penalty.

The visitors took an undeserved lead in the second half when Luke Chadwick tapped home from close range after Nigel Martyn failed to hold a long shot from Ole Gunnar Solskjaer, and the scene was set for a frantic finale as we battled to get something from the game. Mark Viduka's spectacular flying header from Danny Mills's right-wing cross at least dragged us back on to level terms, but we weren't satisfied with that. We wanted a victory, and we thought we had it when Wes Brown turned Lee Bowyer's low, driven cross into his own net. The offside flag that denied us was incorrect. I still maintain, looking at the overall picture of our season, that being deprived of those three points that day effectively prevented Leeds from claiming a place in the Champions' League in 2001–02. It was, then, a decision that cost us many millions of pounds.

A match like that inevitably provokes debate, but given Sir Alex's observations about stamping meriting a red card, you can imagine my surprise when word arrived in Madrid forty-eight hours later of the great man's press conference at Manchester Airport as his team were heading to Athens for their Champions League clash with Panathinaikos. Apparently he had changed his mind and decided that the problem at Elland Road was not that Barthez had stamped on Harte, but that Harte was 'a diver'.

I have a massive respect for Fergie in many ways, not least his approach to disciplinary issues. He always insists on looking after matters internally without any intervention from outsiders, be they media men or rival managers. He deals with things privately and his players can rely on that. Incidentally, I also like Alex's brother Martin, who scouts for the Mancunians, very much. He is a fine man who has coped with testing family tragedies in the most inspirational manner. But however much I respect Sir Alex, like him, I won't tolerate anyone saying anything against my players, or interfering in the affairs of Leeds United.

I was tipped off that the English media would want a response to Sir Alex's comments. Obviously I was surprised by his U-turn over the Barthez issue, but far from launching a full-frontal verbal assault on Fergie, the truth, which anybody who was at that press conference in the Bernabeu Stadium can confirm, is that what I said was very much tongue in cheek. I smiled as I answered the inevitable question. 'First of all, I only like talking about my players.' Because if anybody slags off my players, I'll protect them just as I would expect Alex to protect his. I then suggested that perhaps, since he was fifty-nine, Sir Alex had forgotten what he had said forty-eight hours earlier about Barthez. Knowing that Sir Alex is the absolute master at creating headlines to suit his cause or to deflect attention away from himself or his club, I added: 'It smells of some sort of smoke-screen to me, though I couldn't tell you what it is. But who am I to compete with the great man?'

There was no hint of malice in my comments. At worst they were mischievous, but I honestly don't believe Alex would hold that against me. Everybody at that press conference smiled warmly and understood that there was no lingering resentment. Sadly, the journalistic demands of the day saw the story change direction. In their eagerness to drum up a back-page lead, the newspapers dispensed with the facts and created a fantasy scenario in which, according to one national, David O'Leary had 'rounded on Sir Alex Ferguson' and we were now, claimed another, locked in 'a furious bust-up'.

I had more important things on my mind, notably the small matter of a game against the reigning champions of Europe, but the next day I was a little surprised to see that, out in Athens, Sir Alex seemed to be continuing to voice Manchester United propaganda with the zeal of an evangelist. Suddenly, the entire disciplinary record of his club was being cited in his defence. As one leading newspaper put it: 'Alex Ferguson has refused to back down in his war of words with Leeds manager David O'Leary.' Well, by this stage, if it was a war of words, it was a one-sided one, because I'd lost interest.

Back in England, aside from a couple of quiet conversations

with my staff about what Sir Alex was playing at, I forgot about the whole thing until, four weeks later, it reared its head while I was on holiday in Dubai during a break in the season for internationals. In Dubai I had a day out at a major horse race meeting and Sir Alex, a keen racing man, was there too. Strolling down to the unsaddling enclosure with the leading trainer David Loader, I ran into Alex. I was taken aback when David, who is a Manchester United fan, said hastily: 'I hope you two are talking.' Alex and I may have differing opinions, but there was no reason for us not to be speaking to each other. Unfortunately, it seemed that David had fallen for the 'Fergie feud' line being churned out by the media. There was no 'feud' between me and Sir Alex, and never has been. We just stood there and had a chat. Inevitably, on my return I was asked during a press conference at Leeds about my encounter with the Old Trafford boss. I replied: 'It was a lovely week and I bumped into Alex and said hello. He was in good form because he really likes his racing, and anybody from Ireland likes racing.' That was it. So you can imagine my exasperation when a couple of journalists tried to make something of this casual meeting by claiming: 'David O'Leary has healed his rift with Sir Alex Ferguson in Dubai.'

The rivalry between Leeds and Manchester United fans is well documented, but at board, management, coaching and playing level there are no problems between us. In fact, there is a definite mutual respect. But given the animosity between the supporters, the last thing we needed was for the press to maliciously invent a war between the two managers.

Whenever we meet at games, Sir Alex and I enjoy a glass of wine or a cup of tea together. On one occasion a couple of years ago when he came to Elland Road, I saw him before the match and invited him to join me for a cup of tea. I got distracted for a moment and lost track of him, so I went hunting for him. I couldn't find him anywhere. Eventually I went to the hospitality room I use for my guests and discovered him sitting between my mum and dad, chatting away to them about life in general. They were all getting along like a house on fire. That's the other side of the man. In a football context, he may be a hard man, but he also has a charming side.

There is no doubt that Alex is singleminded. People cite the example of him dropping Jim Leighton for the 1990 FA Cup final as the ultimate evidence of his ruthless streak. Alex had nurtured Jim's career at Aberdeen before bringing him south. He obviously knew Jim and his family very well, and it must have been a savage blow to the Scotland international to discover that he had been dropped for the replay of the final against Crystal Palace. But however heartbreaking it was for Jim, to me, that was Alex being a good manager. He wanted his team to win the FA Cup, and he couldn't allow himself to be swayed by sentiment. He thought Les Sealey would do a better job, so he had to take the tough decision to leave out Jim. It might have been ruthless management, but sometimes good management has to be ruthless.

Alex has described that selection decision as 'pure animal instinct'. I bet it wasn't the most difficult choice he has made in his professional life, but just imagine the flak Fergie would have faced if Sealey had made a hash of his big chance and handed a couple of goals, and the FA Cup, to Palace. As it was, the manager helped his club to win the FA Cup in 1990. And that trophy was especially important, because it was the first of Fergie's reign and therefore represented the breakthrough he had been working towards for over three years.

In my opinion, Alex is the greatest manager of the modern era. Indeed, his record speaks for itself. He has always attempted to send out his side to play with style. He knows the virtues of solid defending and building a team from the back, but he has also accommodated the sort of attacking play that Manchester United love to see from their club. He will

140

doubtless prove to be the last of the line of managers whose domination involved an element of fear. George Graham was another example of the breed, and he had a similar impact at Highbury. To them the fear factor was healthy, but nowadays you can't run a club on the basis that the players will stay hungry because today's footballers are very wealthy, and they're going to get wealthier. You're dealing with multimillionaires who gain security for life early in their careers. They all want to have paid off their mortgages by the time they're thirty-five.

The press created more mischief at the end of the season during the political row at Old Trafford over Sir Alex's future at the club after the expiry of his manager's contract in the summer of 2002. A report appeared in a Sunday newspaper that often features first-person articles by Sir Alex which, completely out of the blue, catapulted me into the debate. Written by a journalist known to be one of Alex's inner circle, it alleged that I was involved in clandestine talks with Manchester United officials about the manager's job and that Brian Kidd was acting as the secret broker of the deal in the hope of returning to Old Trafford with me as my number two.

This time I was not amused, I was angry. I didn't know anything about who Alex's successor might be. The story was absolutely and categorically without foundation. This journalist friend of Alex's was dragging me into a situation that had nothing to do with me and slinging mud at me into the bargain. I was particularly annoyed that members of the Leeds management team, all committed to the Elland Road cause and on long-term contracts, were being used as pawns in this dirty game. I spoke to my solicitor, Michael Kennedy, about it. Michael, who also represents several Manchester United players, knows Alex well and asked him to call me. But given that there were no direct quotes from anyone in the article it was difficult to know how to nail the rumours.

Alex duly telephoned and left a message on my mobile phone.

I rang him back on my way to the League Managers' Association annual dinner in Nottingham and we had a long chat. I told him I just couldn't understand any of this and assured him that Kiddo had no dealings with Manchester United. Alex said that he didn't know what was going on among the Old Trafford hierarchy and that there must be some kind of hidden agenda to these claims. That weekend the rumour flying around in football was that Alex was on the brink of walking out on United. There were those who were under the impression that he had been ready to do so after his team played Tottenham in their final game of the season that Saturday. He had already sanctioned the departure of his assistant manager, Steve McClaren.

Alex assured me that he had had no involvement in the article that maligned Brian and me, and said he was sorry that we had been dragged into Manchester United politics. I ruefully accepted his apology. We concluded our conversation on cordial terms. I asked him where he was going for the summer and we wished each other a pleasant rest.

You can't stop general speculation about jobs, of course, or genuine approaches, but I want to stay at Leeds for as long as Peter Ridsdale wants me there. The Manchester United rumours had no basis in reality, but a couple of people in Italy had sounded me out during the season. When we played AC Milan I met a high-profile Italian agent who asked me about my Leeds contract. It seemed that Lazio had been inquiring about me in their search for a long-term replacement for Sven-Göran Eriksson. The agent asked to meet me again in Rome when we were over for our game against Lazio, but I really didn't feel I had enough experience, or had got anything like close enough to fulfilling my ambitions in England, to even consider taking my services elsewhere. I am trying to build something at Leeds, and I haven't achieved my goals there yet.

One offer I had accepted from Lazio was the invitation

extended before our Champions League match at Elland Road by one of the club's directors to go to Rome for the Lazio–Roma derby at the Olympic Stadium. I went with one of the Leeds directors and Lazio looked after us both royally. Sven-Göran Eriksson and his assistant, Tord Grip, did everything they could to make it a great trip. They dealt with all the arrangements for us and Sven made a booking for us at his favourite restaurant in Rome. Even when we were on our way to the stadium Tord was on the phone making sure that everything was all right.

I suppose it was that Sunday evening that I fully appreciated for the first time the impact Leeds had made in Europe. As I collected my tickets, some Lazio fans recognised me and began to applaud me. One of them shook me by the hand and actually addressed me as 'Maestro O'Leary'. I'd been called many things in my football career, but never 'maestro'. It was a great compliment. The derby was, as I had been assured, unforgettable. The atmosphere was literally crackling: there were so many firecrackers going off that I thought the stadium was going to be set alight. Fire engines were stationed at both ends of the pitch to douse those thrown on the running track by noisy supporters.

Switching Brian Kidd to first-team coaching duties has been of enormous benefit to Leeds, and our professional relationship has clearly made a big impression outside the club, too, because just before our Champions League semi-final I was approached by a respected agent asking whether Brian and I would be interested in working together at Inter Milan. I was assured that the overture was legitimate and that Inter seriously wanted to know how I felt about it. It was very flattering, but again I made it clear that my ambitions were linked to Leeds United and I wasn't interested in moving abroad. Valencia coach Héctor Cúper was also on Inter's shopping list, and it was he who eventually took the job. The approach did leave me with one immediate problem, though: I had already arranged to go on a scouting mission to watch an Inter player in the Milan derby later that week, and I realised it might look as if I had gone to the game in the hope of bumping into the Inter hierarchy. If the story had broken in the Italian press it would have been very embarrassing for everybody and I would have been caught in the middle.

I realise how lucky I am to have Brian on my staff. You can see the regard in which he is held by the players, and in my opinion, there are few, if any, better coaches in world football. He also helps me to develop my own knowledge. I want people around me who will push me, question me and improve me, and Brian is excellent at that. After all, he has done everything there is to do in the game.

Socially, we don't live in each other's pockets, though I enjoy Brian's company when we get together with our wives. But I have immense respect for Brian the person. He is as trustworthy as they come, and there is no edge to him. In many ways he could have been a priest, he is that good a human being. I hope he doesn't retire from football before I do, because I want him alongside me as my coach for the rest of my managerial career.

I was discussing the quality of our squad with Brian, one of the best judges of players in the business, at our training ground in July 2001. We had just been watching one of the training sessions that emphasise the qualities of Rio Ferdinand, the diamond we bought from West Ham. Brian turned to me and said: 'I don't care what you paid for Rio – he's worth double. That boy is real class, and I mean class of the highest order.' At the time of our recruitment of Rio from West Ham in that £18 million deal we were branded in some quarters as 'crazy', it was good to have the approbation of someone whose opinion is so valuable.

Arsenal manager Arsène Wenger, for one, wasn't slow to condemn the Leeds United transfer initiative. He claimed that the turmoil surrounding the future of the transfer market made our investment too risky and that we might live to regret our high-profile gamble.

I didn't set the fee we paid for Rio. Peter Ridsdale did that in his negotiations with his West Ham counterpart Terry Brown. But I did tell Peter that of all the players I was interested in back in the summer of 2000, Rio was my top priority. I knew we needed a centre back, I wanted the best and the only answer was to persuade the King of Peckham, Rio Ferdinand, to move north.

I can tell you that it was no gamble signing Rio, even for a fee that was, at the time, a world record for a defender and the most expensive price tag in British football history. Brian was absolutely right. As a professional footballer, Rio is flawless. At Leeds we have some top-quality athletes as well as gifted footballers, who take great pride in making training sessions competitive, but Rio is outstanding. Ask him to run in pre-season training and he burns up 100 metres, 150 metres and 300 metres as if his immediate goal is not winning the Premier League title but appearing in the Olympic games. He has that turbocharged power that allows him to change gear and burn off the opposition just when they appear to have the long-legged defender in their sights.

But painting a picture of Rio merely as a great athlete does him a disservice. He is much more than that. Throw a ball in his direction and you realise he is a wonderfully talented player of immaculate touch and technique. Eddie Gray, my assistant manager, insists that he could play anywhere if required. Eddie waxes lyrical about Rio the midfielder, Rio the striker and particularly rates the potential of Rio the wide right player.

Before the transfer negotiations we had accumulated a lot of information on Rio and he was without question the best young centre back in the country. As if to drive home the point, he played magnificently against us in the final game of the 1999–2000 season at Upton Park. I spoke to Peter Taylor, the former England coach, about Rio, not just to gain another insight into his footballing talent but to find out more about Rio the person. Peter told me that Rio had been brought up the right way and had good personal standards. He also told me that he had a burning desire to be the best, and to be acknowledged as the best. It was just what I wanted to hear.

A manager's role in transfer negotiations and the fixing of fees is a highly debated issue and, in some respects, tinged with controversy. We have a clear working practice at Leeds. With help from my backroom and scouting staff, I nominate the players I want the club to sign and my chairman acts as chief negotiator on Leeds United's behalf. I have a fantastic rapport with Peter. When I spoke to him about Rio, he asked me about how I would deploy him in our side. Peter was aware of the view expressed by some that Rio couldn't operate in a back four, that he needed to be the spare defender in a three-man central defensive unit. I was convinced that he would be a massive success in a back four. I'm not infallible, of course, but after twenty years as a top-flight centre back, I reckon I can spot the strengths and weaknesses of defenders. I told Peter we could make Rio an even better player. He's good on the ball, good in the air and quick.

Throughout the summer of 2000 there was speculation that Rio was leaving West Ham. One newspaper story would suggest he was joining Leeds, another that his destination was Old Trafford or Stamford Bridge. Then the Spanish market was reported to be opening for him, with Barcelona and Deportivo La Coruña competing for his services. Needless to say, like most press speculation, it all proved unfounded as Rio began the season once again sporting the claret and blue of West Ham.

I didn't have sleepless nights worrying about whether Rio was joining us, because I knew that my chairman would not let him slip through his fingers without a fight. It was simply a question of Peter timing his approach to West Ham at the opportune moment and being ready when the East London club decided to cash in on their prize asset. Rio played against us at Elland Road on 18 November. He was absolutely brilliant and a key factor in their 1–0 victory.

Allan Leighton, the vice-chairman of the Leeds Uniteds plc board, was also keen to nail down a deal with West Ham, and Peter got to work in the boardroom with the West Ham people at that match. As we all headed home that night, the chairman quietly told me that he thought he was on the brink of a major deal. I was delighted. Lucas Radebe had given the club marvellous loyal service over the years, but in recent times he had been increasingly troubled by his knee injury. Our medical people eventually diagnosed it as a chronic problem for which there was no cure, and there was nothing for it but to nurse Lucas through training and matches and deal with him on a day-by-day basis. Jonathan Woodgate was at the opposite end of the age scale, and should have been actively working towards a lengthy career at the peak of his profession representing club and country, but the trial that cast its long shadow over the club was only a couple of months away, and if Woody was found guilty he could be facing a period of imprisonment and I would be left with a defensive crisis.

At the start of the week that Rio's recruitment was being negotiated at boardroom level, I was preparing for our Champions League clash with Real Madrid, and then had to dash off to Dublin to be at my father's bedside while he underwent his major heart operation. So I didn't know how the Rio talks were going until the Friday, when Peter Ridsdale called me to say he had clinched the deal – at £18 million. I had thought we might have to pay £12 million, or even £15 million, but £18 million? I was staggered.

Fair play, though, to Peter Ridsdale and the board. They had listened when I had insisted that Rio was the man we needed, and were prepared to back my judgement and the belief we all had in our club by pushing out the financial boat to buy him. I was thrilled to have Rio on board. We were introduced on the Sunday, before our game against Arsenal. I met his mum, Janice, who seemed a very nice woman who had instilled good values into her son. I'm told she walked down the tunnel to the edge of the pitch when Rio strode out to greet the fans for the first time before the kick-off. She was overjoyed to see the 40,000 crowd rising to acclaim Britain's most expensive footballer, and a few tears rolled down her cheeks.

Rio reported for training the next day. There is a great environment at Leeds which makes it easy for new players to settle in, and Rio is a smashing lad, a very solid individual. I liked the way he conducted himself. He was young and ambitious and clearly loved West Ham, but he never played the big shot. He showed good manners in dealing with people and recognised that he had joined a group of like-minded young players who were desperate to fulfil their ambitions as a team. Rio loves talking football, and he can't gather enough information in his quest to be the best. He just loves the game.

He made his debut the following weekend at Leicester City. Selection was complicated because we had an away game against Lazio of Rome the following week, and I thought about resting Lucas Radebe so that he would be ready for the Champions League. (Rio was ineligible for European combat at this point.) I also considered playing three centre backs at Filbert Street – Rio, Woody and Lucas. I didn't want to have Rio operating as a sweeper; I saw a system that would allow us to use all three centre backs with four midfielders working in front of the trio.

That's what I went for in the end, but before the first half was over we found ourselves three goals down and the plan was in disarray. It wasn't Rio or the system that was at fault: Woody had given away two goals through sheer sloppiness. I don't think he had prepared properly for the game, because his concentration wasn't sharp enough. Leicester had scored from two set plays with which he had been specifically deputed to deal in an agreed way and he failed to do that. I took Woody off and changed our defence. In praise of Woody, I must make it clear that he responded to my criticism and a few days later produced a masterful performance against Lazio in the Olympic Stadium. His reaction emphasised my belief in his ability.

Back at Filbert Street, we eventually lost 3–1. It could have finished in a 3–3 draw given the chances we had in the second half, but you cannot afford to give any team a three-goal start. The defensive chaos was increased with the dismissal of Lucas in the second half. But it is my honest opinion that Rio did nothing wrong on the day. After a difficult start, he remained composed.

I knew what would happen in the post-match analysis, however. It was inevitable that Rio would be blamed for a three-goal flop, and that kind of assessment was completely unfair and unjustified. But when you're an £18 million British record signing and the most expensive defender in the world, the inquisition after a defeat is certain to centre on you.

Rio joined the club at a difficult time in terms of our form and injuries. People were doubting his ability to play at the highest level for club and country; people who have never had to make a judgement about a player were revelling in the let's-knock-Rio mentality of the time. The great thing about Rio was that he never allowed the size of the transfer fee to get to him. He hadn't set it, so why should he get upset about it?

He proved them all wrong. A few months later people were raving about Rio and saying that his fee was a snip. I had to smile when one of the newspapers that had carried banner headlines declaring that Rio did not deserve that fee announced a few months later that England faced a crisis because Rio was injured and looked likely to miss the pre-season friendly against Holland. In the autumn of 2000 he was a high-risk player prone to costly mistakes; by the summer of 2001 he had become the key player in the England team and his potential absence a national emergency.

I can't see a better central defender in British football than Rio. He has the lot. He wants to learn about football and improve so, with the right attitude allied to his natural ability, he will go from strength to strength and emerge as one of the game's true greats.

9

The Final Trial

Everybody at Leeds United had been well aware for months
that October 2001 would be overshadowed by the second
trial of the Leeds United players in connection with the attack
on Sarfraz Najeib. Yet in many ways, the resumption of the legal
machine in Hull crept up on us. We had started the new football
season in impregnable style. By early October, as the pretrial
legal arguments began, we were top of the Premiership and
unbeaten, having conceded only two goals in our opening seven
games. Those matches, allied to our opening tie in the UEFA
Cup against Maritimo and international commitments for many
of our players, left no pause for reflection in the hectic opening
weeks of the campaign.

Before the pretrial hearing, Michael Duberry had been at the
centre of some intense legal wrangling. During the first trial, he
had eventually been represented by the London solicitors who

were already defending Lee Bowyer. Dubes had been acquitted on the charge of conspiracy to pervert the course of justice, but now found himself in an even more invidious position as he admitted to the court that his original witness statement had been untrue, and declared that he wanted to tell the whole story to clear his own name. In the first trial, the prosecution had attempted to discredit Michael's claims that he was finally telling the truth, even though he knew that it might rebound on his friends and team-mates Woodgate and Bowyer.

For the retrial Duberry had been lined up as a key witness for the prosecution, who were now ready to put him back into the witness box, this time accepting his version of events. This left Michael's lawyers, who were still representing Bowyer, facing a potential conflict of interests. So, at the eleventh hour, Dubes had to switch to a new legal team, also from London. They hoped to persuade the court that it was impossible for him to appear as a witness for the prosecution and that the best course of action would be for his evidence from the first trial to be read out the second time around as a witness statement. I felt sorry for Michael as he went through all this again, especially after the emotional turmoil he had endured in Hull a few months earlier. To make matters worse, Michael knew that because he was not a defendant, his legal costs could not be passed on to the court, and he faced a bill of tens of thousands of pounds simply for obtaining the best advice and representation in court as a potential witness.

His preparations for the new season had been affected, too, by requests for legal briefings in London and Leeds. On one particular occasion he was forced to cry off a behind-closed-doors friendly – a game we had arranged with his lack of match fitness very much in mind – to attend his barrister's chambers in London. I'm not suggesting that football is more important than the law, but as a professional player Michael is sensitive to the demands of his profession. He had been declared an innocent man a few months earlier, yet again he found himself at the epicentre of a legal debate he could do next to nothing to influence.

The pretrial began on Wednesday 3 October in Court 4 of Hull Crown Court, the same modern chamber that had been the stage for the first trial. This time, however, the proceedings were presided over by Mr Justice Henriques. When a new manager takes over at a football club it is only to be expected that the team will discuss his track record, the kind of player he likes and dislikes, the decisions he makes and the strategies he deploys, and it appears that within legal circles there are similar debates about the appointment of a judge. Previous landmark cases dealt with by Mr Justice Henriques, directives he had issued and his awareness of political situations were all mulled over by the lawyers. It would be a gross exaggeration to describe the mood of Bow and Woody as optimistic, but several members of their respective legal teams seemed keen to encourage their belief that the case would be thrown out at the pretrial stage on the grounds of prejudice. The players and club officials were urged to accept that there was no way there could be a fair second trial in view of the publicity and general furore surrounding the abandoned first one. The four defendants this time – Bowyer, Woodgate and Woody's friends from Middlesbrough, Neale Caveney and Paul Clifford – were all seeking to have the retrial halted by Mr Henriques before the jury was sworn in, and the legal arguments presented to the judge were absolutely critical in this campaign.

On the opening day, Mr Henriques did show a sympathetic approach by declaring that during the legal arguments, only the defendant whose case was being discussed need be in the dock. Lee Bowyer's lawyers were first to speak, so Woody and his mates were allowed to leave the court. I have already expressed my belief that during the previous trial Woody's personal welfare had not been best served by separating him from his team-mates in court, or by his unavailability for training. His weight loss had been dramatic and a major cause for concern among our medical staff. This time his attitude was much more positive. We talked about how he would cope and he said that he wanted to train and to play as much as possible, and as a result he had not been nearly as badly affected by nervous tension in the run-up to the pretrial. I was delighted to hear that when he was released from the court on that opening day, he had immediately called coach Roy Aitken at Thorp Arch to tell him that he would be available for the reserve-team match that night at Aston Villa. This was a totally different approach from Woody and he played well alongside Michael Duberry at the heart of our defence in a 2–0 victory.

As the judge made his opening comments to the court, it seemed that his every utterance and action was analysed and assessed as being either pro or anti the defendants. His clear criticisms of the way the first trial had been sabotaged by the *Sunday Mirror*, and of the citation of racism as a reason for the attack on Sarfraz Najeib, for example, were seen by many onlookers as favourable signs for the defendants, especially as Mohammed Najeib, the victim's father, was sitting in court listening to his words. But Mr Henriques made it plain in his early directives that he would not be responding in a piecemeal fashion: only when he had heard the submissions for all four defendants would he announce whether or not the full trial would go ahead.

In the pretrial debate over whether he should give evidence this time for the prosecution, Michael Duberry was again represented by Clare Montgomery QC, the eloquent barrister who had acted for him at the original trial. Ms Montgomery's hectic diary dictated that his part in the proceedings had to be determined on the third day of the hearing. The Duberry decision, and the way Mr Henriques dealt with it, was perceived as a major insight into the prevailing climate. Clare Montgomery bought a day return ticket to Hull from London and did her best to convince the judge that Michael should be spared the ordeal of giving evidence again, only to hear the judge direct against her client. Duberry would have to give evidence or face the consequences – and those consequences were potentially draconian.

The defence teams we heard from at Elland Road saw this as a major setback. 'You can take it there's going to be a second trial,' one of the lawyers told us. But I can say, hand on heart, that I had already decided that there would be. For all the supportive words of some of the solicitors involved, I was never swept away on a tide of optimism. There seemed to me to be a political undercurrent carrying the court proceedings inexorably to one outcome: Leeds United on Trial Part 2. As far as I was concerned, the case was bound to develop into a full trial, no matter what anybody said, however benevolent the judge appeared and however approvingly he nodded at certain moments of the pretrial. And indeed, having heard all the legal arguments, the judge decided that another trial was the only fair way to deal with the case.

It was on the afternoon of Friday 5 October that we heard that Michael had lost his campaign and would have to give evidence. I decided I would speak to him about it at the first opportunity. I was aware that he was telling friends at Hull that he would not and could not testify against his colleagues, and the danger of maintaining this stance was stark: he ran the risk of being sent to prison for contempt of court, and I felt it was important that he fully understood this.

The following day saw the conclusion of England's World Cup qualification programme with the match against Greece at Old Trafford. Many of our players were away on international duty, but the remainder reported for Saturday training at Thorp Arch. I spotted Michael walking through the area by the dressing rooms, and called him over for a chat. I was sensitive to the fact that I could not expect to exert an undue influence on his eventual decision, but I did feel that, as his manager, I had a duty to ensure that he appreciated all the nuances of the situation, the pros and the very definite cons.

Michael seemed happy to discuss the issue with me and made no bones about the fact that he would be maintaining the position he had eventually taken at the first trial and giving evidence to this effect. He had hoped it wouldn't come to this, but now there was no turning back. He had no choice.

It was around this time that Michael, popping into one of the offices at the training ground and sitting down at the table, noticed a transcript of a telephone tape-recording that had been left there. The voicemail message had been received after he had given evidence during the first trial but, like the rest of the obscene and abusive material we had had to deal with, it had been kept out of his sight. It was just an unfortunate coincidence that he happened to come into this particular office while work on a legal statement was underway.

It's incredible that any human being should willingly utter the kind of appalling, racist filth recorded on that tape. The caller had said he was from London, and his accent supported that claim, but of course he hid behind the withheld number facility. He was not abashed, though, by the distress he caused the unfortunate telephonist. Simply rereading that transcript makes me feel ill. And as if the racist taunts were not bad enough, the detailed death threats were another matter. What a brave boy. And his was not the only such call that day.

It is incidents like this that emphasise how hard it was for Michael to give evidence. Not only would he have to deal face to face with Woody, in particular, around the club afterwards, but now he remained in no doubt as to the opinion in which he was held by some psychos in the wide and wonderful world.

In court on 22 October, Michael was asked whether he had 'lied, lied and lied again about your involvement'. He responded: 'Yes, I did not tell the truth to the police.' He said he had lied to cover for his friend and team-mate, Woody, and had then been advised by his solicitor to stick to his story because otherwise he would run the risk of being jailed for perjury.

Dubes had met Woody in City Square, Leeds shortly after Sarfraz Najeib had been beaten up in a nearby street. Earlier that evening, Michael had been playing for the Leeds United reserve side against Liverpool and had driven into the city centre to meet up with some of his team-mates afterwards. According to Michael's evidence, he wandered off from the Majestyk Nightclub and ran into Woodgate on his way back there. He told the court: 'I asked him where he'd been. His words, I think, were, "We've just been in a fight." He mentioned that his mate [Paul] Clifford had bitten someone.'

Duberry then drove Woody and his friends to his home in Woodlesford, Leeds in his black Range Rover. When first questioned by the police, however, he had told them that Woody and his friends had gone to his house by taxi. Clifford admitted that at Duberry's home he changed out of his nightclubbing clothes into a tracksuit provided by Michael because one of his friends, Jamie Hewison, had been sick over him in the car.

On the matter of his blatant lies, Duberry admitted: 'At the beginning it was to help Woody out. Then it escalated into one big story that was not true.' He said that when he arrived at his home with Woodgate, Clifford, Caveney and two others, he had taken a call on his mobile phone from his Leeds team-mate Michael Bridges.

Duberry passed the phone over to Woody so that he could speak to Bridges, but the line went dead. So Duberry rang Bridges back and again gave the phone to Woody, who went out into the hall to take the call. In his evidence Duberry claimed that Woody returned to the room and said: 'The lad's in a bad way. There's an ambulance and police there.' Michael said that his team-mate 'appeared shocked' and that everybody in the room seemed upset. He added: 'I think Clifford took it the worst. Everyone was round him and consoling him. I do not remember what words were said.'

Under cross-examination, Duberry claimed that, having lied to the police in his first witness statement to cover up for Woodgate, he met Peter McCormick, his original solicitor, before his arrest in March 2000 and told him that he wanted to change his version of events to the truth. Asked what Mr McCormick had said, Duberry replied: 'He mentioned perjury and said to stick to what was in my statement.' This was an assertion that Mr McCormick would strenuously deny later in the trial.

David Fish QC, representing Woodgate, asked Michael: 'Are you telling me that your solicitor told you to carry on lying?' Duberry replied: 'Yes.' He went on to explain why he had behaved as he did. 'I would say I am an intelligent person, but you are dealing with lawyers and big words like "perjury" and "prison". It is a scary situation when lawyers are mentioning perjury and prison, and on his advice I stuck to the same statement. I might have been naïve but, right or wrong, that's what I have done.' Duberry had undoubtedly been under a lot of pressure, but if he had told the truth from the outset, all this grief could have been avoided.

Peter McCormick's moment to put the record straight came on 27 November. He told the jury: 'If it were proved that I advised a client in that way, it would be the end of my career and, I suspect, of my freedom as well.' He had first discussed the case with Duberry on 31 January 2000, two weeks after the attack. He said that he asked Duberry on several occasions if he wanted to alter his statement, but the footballer declined and maintained that his statement was true. Indeed, according to Mr McCormick, he met Duberry privately after the West Yorkshire police intimated that they were unhappy with the player's account of how Woodgate and his friends got to his house on the night of the assault. He explained to Duberry that detectives felt that they had not got to the bottom of what happened. 'Michael Duberry told me he had told them everything, and there is no truth whatsoever in the allegation that I encouraged him to lie.'

Mr McCormick denied that Duberry had mentioned anything to him about a conversation with Woodgate concerning 'a fight with Asian lads', one of whom had been bitten. He told Woodgate's QC that Duberry had never said to him – as he had claimed in court – 'I can't go on lying like this.' Mr McCormick pointed out that he had nothing to gain and everything to lose by encouraging Duberry to lie.

The retrial, at which he was called as a witness, was the first opportunity Peter McCormick had to speak out about the sensational testimony Duberry had delivered in the first trial and repeated on his second appearance at Hull Crown Court, because the professional relationship between a solicitor and his client had prevented him from making any statement during or after the first trial, even though Duberry's evidence was potentially damaging to his professional reputation. He now told the court, when asked about the veracity of Duberry's version of their meetings and his advice, 'It was entirely the reverse. It was then that I told him that if he had said anything to the police that was not the truth, now was the time to tell the truth.'

It went largely unnoticed by the court reporters that at the beginning of his testimony Peter McCormick also dealt with an issue that had caused some difficulties for Leeds United FC during the first trial, when he had been described in the press as 'a Leeds director, club solicitor and the director responsible for discipline'. At the time of the attack, however, he was none of those things. So you can imagine the exasperation at Elland Road at the headlines screaming, 'LEEDS UNITED DIRECTOR TOLD ME TO LIE'. But because the misrepresentation had been made in evidence in an ongoing trial, the club, like Peter McCormick, had been powerless to put the record straight.

However, the court now heard from Mr McCormick that he had been a director of the club between 1995 and 1998. He was not the club's solicitor, although his practice was one of a number that undertook work for Leeds United. After standing down from the board, he had been awarded the honorary position of associate director. Since he was often seen sitting alongside the club's hierarchy at games, it was understandable if some of the Leeds players still thought of him as a fully fledged director, but he wasn't; neither was he responsible for discipline. In fact, on the basis of even this tangential connection, Mr McCormick stood down as Duberry's solicitor before the first trial because of the dangers of a potential conflict of interests.

The overwhelming pressure of Duberry's testimony on both himself and Woodgate led perhaps inevitably to the breakdown at last of the relationship between the two players. That is a matter of some sadness given the close bond between them of many years' standing. Even as he gave his 'damaging' evidence for the prosecution against Woody, Michael told the retrial: 'We're still good friends. I just do not want to be here. He has always been my best mate at the club. From the very beginning, I've tried to not to say things that would be damaging to Woody. Then I got to the stage where I would have to help myself even if it damaged Woody. I felt sad, gutted.'

I described earlier how the two centre-backs could be seen laughing and joking their way through life, even after the strain of the first trial. This time, though, things ended very differently. Woody is not the most calculating of people, and perhaps it took time for the full impact of the Duberry evidence to sink in, but sink in it eventually did. He told the court he had made a conscious decision not to speak to Dubes. 'I will on the pitch, and when I am at Leeds, but not off the field. He's no friend of mine. I ignore him. He doesn't care if I go to prison or not.' He

160

branded Duberry a liar concerned only with saving his own skin.

Friends who saw Bow and Woody at Hull Crown Court are unanimous in emphasising the huge physical and mental toll the proceedings took of them. Although during the second trial Woody coped better and battled valiantly to keep going, eventually it all became too much for him again. He tried to turn out for the reserves, but his loss of conditioning was causing a clear deterioration in his performances. Woody isn't a lad who carries spare bulk or muscle, so he if starts shedding pounds, he has a problem. It was so sad to see vastly inferior opponents bouncing him around in reserve-team outings simply because of the ravages of events off the field.

I sensed that the loyalty shown to Jonathan by his agent, Tony Stephens, was a great help to the lad. During the second trial, Tony communicated on a regular basis with club officials in an attempt to plot the best route forward for his client as we assessed the impact of the proceedings and what lay in store for him beyond them. He had a real grasp of the kind of issues Woody would face in the future, whatever the outcome of the trial. But even Tony and his associates couldn't prevent the case from forcing Woody on to the sidelines on matchdays.

Bowyer, on the other hand, had been a tower of strength in the first half of 2001. His form had been so impressive during the first trial that he had deservedly won the 'double' of our Player of the Year and Players' Player of the Year awards. His goalscoring panache and outstanding performances in our Champions League campaign had proved inspirational. Yet the second time around we saw a different side to Bowyer. His form in the early stages of the season was not as sensational as it can be, and then, once the trial had begun, he broke his nose and damaged a hamstring in matches. I know the people close to him at Hull were worried by how depressed he seemed. They knew how important his football was to him, and how cruelly he was inhibited by the hamstring injury, which he picked up against Tottenham on 4 November.

It was also a massive problem for the club's medical staff. Complaining about our inability to treat an injured player who is sitting in the dock accused of serious offences may seem churlish and misguided, but the fact remains that our physiotherapists have to concentrate on keeping players fit. Bow had a tricky injury that would have responded more quickly to intense treatment, but instead of receiving round-the-clock attention he could only be treated outside court hours. Sitting in a courtroom most of the day didn't help his recovery programme, either, but he could hardly have stood up and asked the judge's permission to do some stretching exercises.

The broken nose came in an accidental clash with Nicky Butt in our 1–1 draw at Manchester United on 27 October. It was a bad break that required an operation – he had to be given leave to miss three days of the court hearing for the bone to be reset – but the swelling around the fracture was so pronounced that he had to wait till it went down before he could have the corrective surgery. He was very frustrated by the breathing problems it caused him in the meantime.

When Bow appeared in court after the Old Trafford game, the damage to his nose was obvious and he had the beginnings of a black eye. Before proceedings commenced, Mr Justice Henriques explained to the jury that the player had sustained his injuries during a football match. 'It is right you should know that it was the result of lawful activities and not in a fight anywhere,' he said.

Any worries that Bowyer's declarations of innocence might be undermined by football-related injuries evaporated when he was called to give evidence. It was perhaps no surprise when, under questioning from his counsel, Desmond de Silva QC, Bow insisted: 'I never went into Mill Hill. Not at the start, not during, not at the end. I told the police that from day one.'

It was, of course, in Mill Hill that Sarfraz Najeib had been thrown against an industrial waste bin, beaten, bitten and left semi-conscious on the pavement. And it was under cross-examination by the prosecutor, Nicholas Campbell QC, that Bowyer ferociously defended himself against accusations that he had concocted a clever web of lies. Campbell insisted that Bowyer had 'lurked in the shadows' outside the Leeds night-club before joining in the punching and kicking of Sarfraz Najeib.

'In a calculated manner you have attempted to pull the wool over the eyes of the jury,' he said.

'I am standing here and telling everybody the truth,' retorted Bowyer immediately. The prosecution continued for half an hour to attack Bowyer's recollection of events, to probe for an error in his testimony that could have proved decisive. But Bowyer stood firm. 'I cannot believe I am here,' he said. 'I was never in Mill Hill.'

'You did go into Mill Hill, together with your team-mate Jonathan Woodgate, and joined in the attack on Mr Najeib.'

'I was not involved in any violence that evening.'

'All of you had been in Mill Hill,' persisted Mr Campbell, 'and you made good your escape, but in the middle of that, you could not resist a post-score celebration.' He was referring to an embrace with another of the accused, Neale Caveney, that was caught on closed-circuit TV cameras.

'Mr Campbell, that is rubbish,' said Bowyer.

The prosecutor described this 'victory hug' between Bowyer and Caveney and repeated: 'You could not resist engaging in a post-score celebration. You were being euphoric, Mr Bowyer.'

Lee replied: 'I was not part of any attack and did not injure anyone.' His unyielding stance clearly succeeded in persuading the court that he had not been in Mill Hill that night.

By the time the jury retired to consider their verdict on Monday 10 December, a multitude of reporters and journalists had prepared their pieces on all the defendants, their families and their associates. Some of the gnarled old crime writers who had covered both trials on a daily basis predicted the verdict would be quickly reached. It would take only a day or two, they said.

Mr Justice Henriques told the jury of seven women and five men that he wanted unanimous verdicts. There was a suggestion that if they could not reach these by the Thursday, he might reduce that demand, but decided that he would wait for the unanimous verdicts until the following Monday. On the Friday lunchtime the message was relayed to the judge that the jurors did not have verdicts on all eight charges against the four accused, but were ready to deliver on the issues on which they absolutely agreed.

At this precise moment I was about fifty miles away at Thorp Arch, near Wetherby, holding a press conference prior to our Premier League game against Leicester City two days later. A club official told me: 'Woodgate guilty of affray. Bowyer not guilty of GBH, but the jury will now consider majority verdicts on Woody for GBH and Bow for affray.'

It might sound strange now, but I just carried on with my press conference. I knew the only time to make a considered response would be when we knew all the facts, so I politely asked my inquisitors not to stray from the Leicester game and they accepted my guidelines. That was surreal enough, but if the press had seen what happened next, they would not have believed their eyes.

In the front quadrangle at Thorp Arch all of our staff members were assembling: the famous first-teamers, the laundry ladies, the physiotherapy staff, the personal assistants to the secretariat. They were gathering for our traditional Christmas outdoor concert, featuring performances by youngsters from the Leeds United Academy, followed by a Christmas lunch for all, turkey, the usual trimmings, the lot.

Some of these teenagers are more diffident than others, but

they all sing for their supper – or in this case their lunch. We don't force them to sing solos: we accept group efforts. I act as the compère, introducing the performers, and they launch into festive standards such as 'Rudolph the Red-Nosed Reindeer' and so on. There is no heckling, every rendition is applauded and it's a joy to see the smiles on the faces of the teenagers and the famous stars alike as they celebrate Christmas together.

At this precise moment Jonathan Woodgate was sitting in a cell at Hull Crown Court wondering if he was about to be found guilty of GBH. It must have been a harrowing time for him because the verdict on the more serious charge – the charge that carried a custodial sentence – had not yet been decided. Leeds United had already stated that if any of the players involved in the case were found guilty of this offence they would never play for the club again. Peter Ridsdale had issued that directive before the first trial, and I totally supported his stand.

The wait was around half an hour. Then Woodgate returned to the dock to be told that, by a majority verdict, he had been found not guilty of GBH. And Bowyer, also by a majority decision, was not guilty of affray. So Lee had been acquitted on both charges. Our training ground was deluged with calls from the press asking for our response to the verdicts, but we could say nothing at this point for one clear reason: the judge had yet to hand down Woody's sentence. I sat in an office watching Sky News on television. A reporter was confidently predicting that Woody would be jailed. And it was quite possible. After all, his friend Paul Clifford, who had been found guilty of GBH, was eventually sentenced to six years' imprisonment.

I didn't know what to expect. Throwing the lads out of Leeds was not now on the agenda, but it was still within the judge's power to have Woody locked up. The television reporter, still maintaining that a spell in jail was inevitable, looked quite crest-fallen when news of Woody's sentence came in: 100 hours of community service.

Although Bow walked free, acquitted on both counts, the sting in the tail for him was that the judge believed he had lied to the police and therefore refused to award him costs. So both Bowyer and Woodgate faced massive legal bills.

I have heard from media people all over the country that many newspapers and television and radio companies just didn't know how to react to these verdicts. Hours, days and weeks, even, had been spent on gathering background interviews and writing articles about the Leeds Two, most of which had been compiled on the basis that the boys would be found guilty and would be sent to prison. Suddenly, all that effort seemed to evaporate into virtually nothing. Now legal restrictions would inhibit the media's ability to exploit the situation in which Bowyer and Woodgate might have found themselves. Denied the obvious routes to filling column inches and programme hours, several journalists, still fired up by the feeding frenzy of the afternoon, lashed out in other ways.

One writer who I have known for many years decided to attack the club's decision to play Bowyer and Woodgate during the period after their arrest. He believed that the Football Association was right to impose a suspension until the duo had proved their innocence. The Leeds United stance, of course, was that they were innocent until proven guilty. To my mind, that is a fundamental tenet of English law. I may have vehemently opposed the FA's position, but I was even more annoyed by the way this writer attempted to defend that policy. He drew an outlandish analogy with teachers accused of molesting children being suspended on full pay pending the outcome of their trial. He compared our players with doctors charged with indecently assaulting their patients, policemen indicted for corruption, accountants cited for fraud or lawyers arraigned for misconduct.

Personally, I would add to that list bankers accused of theft and chemists accused of the illegal supply of drugs. But all those people are dealing every day in their business or professional lives with potential victims or other issues directly related to the crimes with which they are charged. You cannot allow a teacher accused of child molestation to continue with his work, because it involves interacting with children on a daily basis; being in close contact with children is a fundamental part of his job.

As for Bow and Woody, their daily professional lives involve reporting to our training ground to work on physical conditioning, practising their football skills and receiving instruction in a number of technical disciplines. Once, twice or occasionally three times a week, they will report to a football stadium to ply their trade in front of an audience. Running around the streets of Leeds in a drunken state is not part of their job descriptions; indeed, by allowing them to continue with their work we are much more likely to be able to eliminate the circumstances that led them into trouble in the first place than we would be by suspending them.

I am very aware that whenever we are talking about these players, about the FA and about issues such as this one, we are likely to be accused of overlooking the suffering of the victim, Sarfraz Najeib. But that has never been the case with me, with Peter Ridsdale or with anybody else at our club. We expressed our disgust at the attack from the moment we first heard about it, and we continue to express our outrage still. As soon as I knew the full picture of this attack, I called all the Leeds players to a team meeting. When I had got them all in front of me, I pointed at Bow and Woody and said: 'These two have disgraced us all. They were running around Leeds drunk that night. The terrible consequence of that evening was that a human being was left lying on the floor as though he was nothing more than a piece of meat.' I was shouting at them. I was absolutely incensed by what had happened.

At one point we had four players facing charges, Tony

Hackworth and Michael Duberry having been acquitted after the first trial. I have spoken to the players about their irresponsible behaviour. I never lose sight of the reality that a man was savagely beaten that night, and when I review the whole depressing episode, I just cannot comprehend how players from Leeds who, week in and week out, are told how to behave, could have become involved in allegations connected with such a brutal attack on a human being.

Their conduct was an utter disgrace, and even though Bowyer and Woodgate were both found not guilty of the more serious charge of GBH, I was still ashamed of them. Everyone at the club from the chairman to the backroom staff has worked hard to build a relationship with our community, only to have it knocked back by sheer stupidity. And Leeds United has much to be proud of in our involvement in the community. We have been shortlisted, for example, for national awards for our anti-racism campaigns in local schools; we have erudite spokesmen on anti-racism issues in the shape of Lucas Radebe, Olivier Dacourt and Mark Viduka. Viduka may be white, but he has plenty of experience of racism, having suffered as a young man in the Balkans because of his Croat roots.

Ever since I took over at Leeds, I have made sure that the players are kept in line in every situation, from staying away in hotels to their treatment of the staff at the club. On only one occasion have I had to reprimand them: when, before a match, they boarded the team coach leaving the hotel room they had been using as a lounge in a mess, with newspapers and sweet wrappers strewn around the place. I refused to allow a member of the hotel staff to clean up after them. Instead I ordered them all off the coach and sent them back to tidy it up. And I've never had to repeat that order.

But no matter how many times you tell players about their off-field behaviour, you can't keep watch over them in their spare time away from the club. They will make their own decisions about their recreational activities. Woody and Bow made bad decisions that night, and no one can imagine just how let down I felt. Whatever the court decided, in my eyes, they were guilty of neglecting to exercise control, of lacking responsibility and of failing to behave as professional athletes. What were they doing boozed up and running through the streets? Was that not inviting trouble? At Leeds we appointed a doctor, Steve McGregor, who specialises in sports science, and he has talked to the players repeatedly about the damage alcohol can do to your body. Steve has a great relationship with our footballers, and I believe that they listen to him. It is unfortunate that he had not yet joined us when the chase and attack took place.

Steve explains to the players that they have to limit their alcohol intake. 'If you must have a drink,' he tells them, 'keep it to a couple of glasses of wine, a quiet drink in a restaurant with your wife or girlfriend with a meal.' The lads must avoid tipping pints of lager down their throats as seems to be dictated by a boozing culture that has developed among British footballers. Why is it you never see foreign players getting drunk, abusing their bodies and hogging the headlines with their misbehaviour? They enjoy themselves with a glass of wine. I'm afraid too many British players seem intent on getting legless. I know of a trophy-winning team whose manager noticed after the celebration of one of their more recent triumphs that the only drunken players in the room were the Brits.

I didn't feel like celebrating the verdicts from Hull. Nobody at Thorp Arch was punching the air that day. There was just a sense of relief that the whole ordeal was finally over. It had lasted for two years, covering three football seasons; two years of intolerable pressure on the club, on my players and on myself.

I have written already in these pages of the hate mail and phone calls we received at the club and of how I was targeted, and so was Peter Ridsdale, as well as the players directly involved in the case, who had plenty of malicious communications. But the correspondent who caused most concern to my staff and me was the one who wanted to get to my wife, someone who has no association with football other than being married to me. He even spelled out how he wanted to kill her. It was this person who forced us to call in the police. We receive mail from strange people all the time, even parcels of dog excrement. Every club does. But this missive was in a league of its own. It was deeply personal.

I have had death threats before. During my days as an Arsenal player, the IRA targeted me. As I recall, they took offence at pictures of me showing Prime Minister John Major and his son around Highbury. A letter arrived from the terrorists and the police believed that the words in it contained a code which suggested that they were serious. I missed Arsenal's next game, and security at my home in north London was stepped up. I remember being shown how to check for bombs placed under our cars and to recognise any hint that our vehicles had been tampered with. We had padlocks on sheds in the garden and the dustbins were checked regularly and locked away.

But these letters that arrived at Leeds made my blood run cold. They seemed to be linked with developments in the trial, or with Woody and Bow making the news with their performances for the club. There was no escaping them. I can't go into too much detail because the police are still investigating them, but each letter was written in the same style by somebody who said that he wanted to kill Joy, and would kill Joy if I included Bow and Woody in the Leeds side.

I was in a quandary. I will admit now that when the first letters came I did not burden my family with them. But when the threats on Joy's life were repeated, and security at the office was tightened up – the staff handling the mail voluntarily provided fingerprints so that the police could attempt to isolate the writer's prints – I knew I would have to put her on her guard.

But I didn't actually tell her that someone was threatening to kill her. I didn't want to terrify her. Why allow a crank the satisfaction of causing chaos and panic in our family? On the day I received the most explicit letter, I went home and found Joy making tea. I told her we'd better step up security around our home and that I wanted her to be a little bit more conscious of who was around her. Joy is a very straightforward woman who doesn't break down in hysterical tears. She just poured the milk into my tea and said, 'OK, fine, I'll do it.'

I weighed up the situation and decided our teenage children, John and Ciara, didn't need to know anything about it. I just took very serious measures to make sure they were safe. Over the past few months the hate mail has continued to arrive. The letters are simply opened, sealed in a sterile plastic bag and handed over to the police.

The tone of the correspondence changed after the terrorist strike on the World Trade Centre in New York on 11 September. A few days afterwards, another letter arrived, introducing a new element. Now, as well as wanting to kill my wife, the crank declared a *jihad*, a Muslim holy war, on me. Of course, in the wake of the atrocities of 11 September, it was a word and a concept that was being bandied about a lot in the media and could have been adopted by anyone. The idea that somebody wanted me dealt with according to such a principle seemed preposterous.

I was brought up a Catholic and continue to attend Mass. My mum goes to ten o'clock Mass in Dublin every day of the week. In church I found myself kneeling and praying for the safety of my wife and children. There I could clear my head and meditate on the issues that really matter. Of all the side-effects of the trial that have challenged and troubled me, I hope that the matter of these letters can be concluded and that their author is brought to justice. Football is football and I want my club to be winners, but my family is my life, and this sick man has tormented me.

There are of course many other issues that require further debate in the aftermath of the court case. For instance, I am aware that the judge will be reporting to the attorney general the circumstances in which an Internet company released to millions of subscribers Mr Justice Henriques's strict guidelines to media outlets on what they could and could not report from the trial. The latter category included, among other things, the names of witnesses who had asked to remain anonymous, the previous criminal records of the accused and details of why the first trial had collapsed. That explosive information was on the world-wide web for three hours before being removed. The next day an executive of AOL was called into court to explain his conduct and the judge established that none of the jurors had read it on their computers at home. AOL apologised, but the damage was already done. A Leeds United Internet fanzine had spotted the material, copied it and put it out on their site inviting comments on their chatlines. The police had to act again to get this bulletin removed. No matter how irresponsibly we feel some sections of the press behave, there are certain guidelines – I won't describe them as principles – that even they must acknowledge, and web-sites, especially the small, low-key ones, are potentially dangerous in spreading confidential information, especially information that is intended to remain within a court of law.

The debate about the trial and, I am sorry to say, many smears and innuendos, have continued since the conclusion of the court proceedings, and I would like to close this chapter with a few facts. The police spoke to more than 1,000 people about the attack on Sarfraz Najeib, taking 499 statements. It has been claimed by some crime journalists that as many, if not more, detectives from the West Yorkshire police force were employed in the detection of this crime as were used in the hunt for the notorious killer Peter Sutcliffe, known as the Yorkshire Ripper.

The two trials in Hull provoked massive publicity. The

intense media focus on the first trial may well have provided background information for the jury at the second hearing six months later. Two skilled judges guided proceedings. At the end of two months spent listening to and considering the evidence, the jury found that Lee Bowyer and Jonathan Woodgate were not guilty of grievous bodily harm. They were not Sarfraz Najeib's attackers. Woodgate was found guilty of being involved in the chase, but no more. These are not matters for debate: they are the verdicts from Hull Crown Court decided on the facts. Yet still it seems many people want to ignore them.

Four days after the trial ended, the club's own punishments for Bow's and Woody's behaviour were announced. The maximum compulsory fine allowed under the guidelines of the players' union, the PFA, is the equivalent of two weeks' wages. It was decided that Jonathan Woodgate should be fined eight weeks' wages and asked to take part in the club's successful community programme. He was also given a final warning regarding his future conduct. Jonathan acquiesced to this penalty, asking for the fine to be put towards our work within inner-city communities, a request we were happy to honour.

In Bow's case, Leeds United acknowledged and accepted the verdict of the jury that he was innocent of all charges, but by his own admission he had been under the influence of alcohol in Leeds city centre that night, and therefore in breach of our code of conduct. The club decided to fine him four weeks' wages, and it was requested that he take a leading role in the Leeds United community programme.

Unfortunately, Lee refused to accept the club's sanctions. He refused to pay any fine and was not prepared to commit himself to any community work over and above that expected of any other first-team player. Consequently he was immediately put on the transfer list and I was asked by the board of Leeds United plc not to select him unless he accepted the club's disciplinary measures.

Epilogue

My flights across the Irish Sea to Dublin during my father's illness have prompted many inquiries about his health and welfare. Dad is absolutely fine now. The O'Leary family will never be able to thank our friend Hugh McCann, his cardiologist, enough for saving my father's life. We will be for ever in his debt.

Having had such direct experience of heart problems I was horrified when Gérard Houllier was taken ill at half-time during our game at Liverpool on 13 October 2001. It's rare for managers to spend much time together before a match, but that day, when I went out on to the pitch shortly after we arrived at Anfield, I was joined by the Liverpool boss. As I have said, I have a lot of time for Gérard and we get on well. He may be ruthless in his decision-making but I think he is totally genuine and I trust him. You can ask his advice about things and never be afraid that he will betray you.

Epilogue

We had a bit of a chat and I told him we were going to kick Liverpool's backsides. He suggested that we met up for a meal the following week with our wives, adding that I had better leave the selection of the wine to him because I had no taste. I thought he looked fine, but he admitted to me that he hadn't been feeling great during the previous month. Gérard loves football and loves his job, but somehow he didn't feel he had the same spark. He said that when he woke up each morning he just didn't seem to have the drive to get going.

I had no idea what had happened that day until the game was almost over. I was just puzzled about where Gérard had disappeared to during the second half. It wasn't until about ten minutes from the end that our substitute Gary Kelly said he'd heard a whisper in the crowd that Gérard had suffered a heart attack at half-time. I was stunned. Afterwards I went to see the Liverpool assistant manager, Phil Thompson, to establish exactly what had happened and asked whether I could go to the hospital to see Gérard. I was told that it wouldn't be a good idea.

The next day I made contact with Gérard's wife, Isabelle, at around seven o'clock in the morning. She explained that it hadn't been a heart attack but that Gérard was suffering from a major heart valve problem that had required immediate surgery. He had only a 20 per cent chance of surviving the operation. I went over to the hospital in Liverpool the same morning. Gérard had just come out of theatre after eleven and a half hours and had been transferred to intensive care. Isabelle was with him. As I waited outside for her, it hit home how seriously ill he was.

When she emerged, Isabelle invited me to go in with her to see Gérard. After my Dad's operation I knew what to expect, so I wasn't shocked, but it was obvious to me that the surgery he had undergone had been extremely serious. He was still unconscious. However, by the time I returned the following day,

Gérard was drifting in and out of consciousness and was able to recognise us. Everyone was delighted with his progress.

I don't think Gérard himself helped his own general health. He was perhaps carrying a touch too much weight and not getting enough exercise. The surgeon who performed his life-saving operation told me that Gérard would be fine because of the success of that amazing surgery, but he added that Gérard would have to change his lifestyle. And he knows he owes that to his wife and family as well as to himself. He worked all hours and yet didn't sleep well. I'm not a great sleeper, either, as I've said – I'm lucky if I get six hours a night – but I do work out and I am not a big drinker. I am also fortunate in that two of my closest friends are a heart surgeon and a GP, so they keep an eye on me. But I do wish I could sleep better.

There have been many occasions when I have been heading home from a night match, at maybe one or two in the morning, and the carphone has rung and it has been Gérard. He's like an owl, working away at night. He'd be calling just to talk about our match and Liverpool's fixture the following night.

We finally had that meal Gérard had suggested on the day he was taken ill when he was recuperating, but instead of going out to a restaurant Joy and I were entertained *chez* Houllier in Liverpool, along with Gérard's brother Serge. Gérard and Isabelle laid on some superb Krug champagne, some beautiful red wine and their great company.

I took along a gift for him, a golf putter, along with a machine that flicks the ball back to you if your putt goes into the hole. I had decided that I should encourage Gérard to take an interest in something outside football, and I thought a putter might kindle his enthusiasm for golf. He had often asked me about the game, and about what I saw in it. I'd tell him it was relaxing, that it got me away from the mobile phone and out into the fresh air, and gave me the kind of break from the stresses and strains of football that a manager needs. It's a great way to enjoy

176

some sort of release in our job, even if as soon as you get back into the car you have about fifteen messages to deal with. At the same time as I was having a break in Dubai last year – in Al Maha, a wonderful place in the desert, probably one of the most peaceful places on the planet – Gérard was taking a holiday in the Seychelles. I had just climbed out of the shower in my hotel room when my mobile rang. It was Gérard. He was calling from the Seychelles to discuss football and to tell me that at the place where he was staying there was a wonderful golf course with a professional who was a Leeds United fan. 'Why don't you start playing golf and give yourself something to do?' I asked him.

I have my golf, Sir Alex Ferguson has his love of horse racing, but I don't think Gérard had anything that provided him with some respite from football. Alex's critics claim that he has taken his eye off the Manchester United job because of his outside interests, but I don't believe that is true at all. I think Alex is obsessed with winning, and that having a hobby that takes his mind off football for a short while probably helps him to cope with the pressures of the managerial game.

Gérard and I agreed at dinner that night to fix a date in the New Year to take our wives to Paris for a long weekend. We might even take a Monday off: you never know. We'll let the women shop, but I bet Gérard will want to visit the Paris St Germain training complex of which he always speaks so highly.

At about quarter past one in the morning, as Joy and I drove home, with the rain beating down on the car, my phone rang. I knew who it would be. 'Thanks for a great night,' said Gérard. 'I'm just practising with my putter and I'm doing quite well. I think I could be good at this.'

Beginners' luck, I'd call it.